WOMEN AND THE ENVIRONMENT

WOMEN AND THE ENVIRONMENT

A Reader
Crisis and Development in the Third World

Edited by Sally Sontheimer

MONTHLY REVIEW PRESS
NEW YORK

Library of Congress Cataloging-in-Publication Data
Women and the environment: a reader: crisis and development in the
   Third World/edited by Sally Sontheimer.
        p. cm.
    ISBN 0-85345-835-9: $13.00
    1. Women in development – Environmental aspects – Developing
countries.   2. Economic development – Environmental aspects
I. Sontheimer, Sally Ann.
HQ1240.5.D44W64   1991
305.42 – dc20

Monthly Review Press
122 West 27th Street
New York, N.Y. 10001

Typeset by Bookman Ltd, Bristol
Printed and bound by Cox & Wyman Ltd

10 9 8 7 6 5 4 3 2 1

CONTENTS

INTRODUCTION

Sally Sontheimer

Over the last twenty years, the relationship between women and the living systems which support their life has changed drastically in response to heavy ecological stress in many areas of poor, developing countries. Like the Sahelian woman who laments the "going of the trees", rural women throughout the Third World look to the past as a time in which the bounty of nature could provide for their needs. Today rural women have inherited a situation where their rights and access to cultivable land have decreased and the open forest, woodlands and bush from which they gather such vital necessities as fodder, fuelwood and water have grown scarce or have disappeared.

There is a commonly held belief that women are responsible for much of the environmental destruction taking place in rural areas. They are seen carrying the heavy loads of wood on their heads and foraging for the last twig or bit of green in areas which have been stripped bare of vegetation. But laying the blame on women is to ignore the globally linked causes of environmental destruction which have created and continue to create a situation of scarcity that often forces women into ecologically destructive actions.

Throughout the developing world, ecological equilibrium has been broken by a number of interacting factors, many of which are the direct result of development policies geared toward survival in the global economy. For most developing countries, economic survival has meant providing the raw natural products and agricultural commodities demanded by markets in the developed countries, often at the cost of widespread natural resource depletion. Economic policies have supported the massive conversion of bush and woodland for agricultural development, the indiscriminate use of water resources for irrigation, the felling of the forests for wood products, and the privatization of once commonly held land. The World Bank, for example, has estimated that 70 per cent of deforestation in Africa is due to the conversion of woodlands to agricultural uses, yet the Bank encourages this result with its support of export agriculture.

These changes in land use and distribution have drastically short-changed the poor, leaving them with not only less access to land, but less fertile land. At the same time, population growth continues to increase the number of people who depend on dwindling resources. The impact of scarcity has been particularly hard on women, who are traditionally responsible for gathering wood and water, making those tasks increasingly arduous and time consuming in a day already burdened by long hours of work. Because women's needs are always the last to be considered within the community and within the family, they are overlooked by development projects which might bring assistance and they always receive the least when scarce resources such as land are being allotted.

Another phenomenon which has been given little attention is the growing number of women left behind on the farm to carry the burden of family survival alone because the men have gone in search of work in urban areas. For the women who have also migrated to the cities with their particular environmental problems of pollution, poor housing and sanitation, poverty brings another kind of hardship. Rarely have women been asked what they think, but surely they would say that "life has become hard".

This book is an effort to tell the too often untold story of women living in the face of ecological distress in developing countries. The book consists of a collection of essays which explore the complex interrelationships that have developed between women and their ecological base of survival, and look at how Third World women are responding to that situation. It was designed to bring together a broad selection of information from the available literature to provide an overview of the current situation.

Behind the selection of the articles was also the perceived need to understand women's role within the overall context of environmental problems in the Third World in order to counter some common misperceptions about the causes of ecological degradation which have often pointed an accusing finger at women. By exploring the larger scenario of changing land use patterns throughout the Third World and the fundamental question of women's right to land, the essays selected for this book seek to provide a complete picture of a reality in which women are less the cause of environmental destruction than victims of a cycle of events beyond their control.

However, the predominant theme that emerges from a reading of the literature is not of women as victims of ecological crises, but rather the extraordinary ability of women to organize themselves to fight ecological destruction and carry out actions that both improve their lives and make a significant contribution to local community development. The stories of women's mobilization for the environment have several elements in common, foremost among them the courage women have shown in the face of two battles which must be fought simultaneously: one against the growing ecological degradation that surrounds them and one against traditional power structures that subordinate their needs within the family and within society. Their victory is obtained through organization, by working together and by uniting their voices to demand that both their rights and nature be treated justly.

The motivation for their actions is based on the full recognition that without a healthy environment, there is no life. We can hear this affirmation of life in the words of the many women which are recounted throughout this book, simple words that express their concern for local ecological problems and a philosophy of living with nature rather than against it. This book seeks to relay a sense of that philosophy because it has proven to be a powerful and valid factor in mobilizing actions and new approaches for a more sustainable use of natural resources. What might then have been a book about tragedy is actually a book about hope.

The book is divided into four sections corresponding to four major themes of discussion. The first three sections present articles which provide an overview of women's use and management of life-sustaining systems – i.e. land, forests and water. All of the essays in the first three sections take a critical look at current environmental projects and their lack of attention to women as beneficiaries and primary agents in ameliorative actions. The last section of the book chronicles but a few of the many examples of women's initiatives, both spontaneous and guided, which are taking place worldwide. The essays in this section recount important success stories of women who have organized themselves to improve their lives and that of their communities through environmental protection or repair.

The first article of the anthology, written by Irene Dankelman and Joan Davidson, looks at the critical issue of land, the food crisis and women's role in agriculture. Here, the central problem is women's lack of legal rights to land and control over land resources. The essay concludes with three case studies that illustrate sustainable agricultural methods practised by women.

The question of women's land rights is brought into sharp relief in Marie Monimart's study of "Women in the Fight Against Desertification". The first part of the study analyses the role women play in desertification control in six Sahelian countries approaching the question of desertification from the women's viewpoint revealing not only the ecological impact but also the enormous socio-cultural changes that have accompanied ecological degradation. One major impact on women's lives has been the departure of the men, which has resulted in greater responsibility and more work without the security of land rights. The second part of the study analyses how anti-desertification projects have involved women and looks at some positive experiences of women's initiatives in anti-desertification measures.

The third essay is part of a project carried out by the Social Forestry Department of the Food and Agriculture Organization of the UN to create a publication on the role of women in forest resource use and management. The essay describes the importance of forest products for women to meet basic needs and provide a source of income, looks at the effects of deforestation on women and their families, analyses the impact of forestry projects on women and offers suggestions to policy makers and development workers on how to formulate projects that assure both women's participation and project success.

The overview on women and forest resources is followed by

a more in-depth look at the cooking energy crisis which is of particular importance for women. "Under the Cooking Pot", by Bina Agarwal, analyses the fuelwood crisis in South Asia. Most importantly, it explores the causes of the crises which are connected to indiscriminate forest exploitation, clearing of land for agriculture and the privatization of common property resources and looks at the impact of these broad trends in land use patterns on the poor. The article also looks at the experience of various tree-planting schemes which in general have failed to address local needs for forest products.

Women's present and potential role in water use and management is the focus of the fifth essay, prepared by the United Nations International Research and Training Institute for the Advancement of Women (INSTRAW), which has been a lead organization during the UN International Drinking Water Supply and Sanitation Decade carrying out research and training on the issue of women and water. The article examines how water supply and sanitation programs have often failed by ignoring women and suggests ways of enhancing women's participation and thereby the success of water-related development projects.

The last section of the book, with its focus on women's initiatives, opens with two case studies on women's mobilization in urban areas of Latin America. Caroline Moser provides a brief introduction to the issue of human settlements with their particular environmental, infrastructural and land use problems which affect women's ability to provide shelter for their families under adverse conditions. Her study of Guayaquil highlights the importance of women in mobilizing the community to upgrade their housing and press the government to provide necessary infrastructures. Frances Dennis and Dulce Castleton provide a study of the Guarari Community Development Project in Costa Rica where women have pioneered a type of community development which combines low-income housing with efforts to protect and restore the natural environment.

The last two stories come from India, which has been the site of two well-known examples of women's mobilization for the environment: Chipko and the rehabilitation of "wastelands". Shobita Jain provides us with a chronicle of the development of the Chipko movement which began as a string of spontaneous confrontations made by village women to stop forest exploitation throughout the Himalayan region of India and which has matured into a feminist, ecological movement. The Bankura story, written by Nalini Singh for the International Labour Organization, is the story of another movement which started in a small village in West Bengal where a women's "samity" obtained degraded "wasteland" and carried out a successful project of tree planting and silk worm production. Both of these experiences have brought women together not only to fight for environmental protection but also to secure women's right to land and to economic and social status.

Note

This reader has been originally prepared by Sally Sontheimer for the Italian Association for Women in Development (AIDoS), with financial contribution from the European Economic Commission.

AIDoS in a non-governmental organization expressly concerned with promoting the role of women in the development process. Its portfolio includes a wide range of activities that can be clustered in three major areas: information and networking, research and training, implementation of development projects in the field. Its main concerns are: women's health, environment, small enterprises and the establishment of information-documentation centres for women.

I

WOMEN AND LAND

LAND: WOMEN AT THE CENTRE OF THE FOOD CRISIS
Irene Dankelman and Joan Davidson

Land, particularly healthy soil, is the foundation on which life depends. If the land is healthy, then agriculture and pasturage will yield food in plenty. If it is not, the ecosystem will show signs of strain and food production will become more difficult. Because women are at the centre of world food production – producing more than 80 per cent of the food in some countries – any analysis of land resources must include an appreciation of their central role.

LITTLE FOOD, NO LAND

The present world food situation is one of the great modern paradoxes: about 500 million people – the largest number ever – are seriously malnourished, while world food production has reached the highest levels in history.

Hunger in the Third World is not necessary. Official Food and Agriculture Organization projections show that the earth can provide more than enough food not only for our present population of 5,000 million, but also for the 6,100 million people expected by the year 2000 (FAO, 1981). But these numerical calculations do not take account of the problems of food distribution, of economic control over food resources, and the politics of food dependency. Access to food is not simply a question of land availability, but of social, political and economic power. The poor have none of these.

Expanding cropland will offer only a limited solution to the landlessness of the poor. Success would depend upon good-quality land being available to those most in need. Of the world's 13,250 million hectares of land, about 30 per cent is estimated to be arable, half of which is now under cultivation. Just over half of the land presently under cultivation is found in developing countries, but it is inhabited by three quarters of the world's population. Within countries, there is severe inequity of land ownership (see Figure 1).

Figure 1: *The landless and near-landless as a percentage of total rural households*

Boliva	85%	Ecuador	75%
Guatemala	85%	Peru	75%
Indonesia (Java, 1971)	85%	Brazil	70%
El Salvador	80%	Dominican Republic	68%
Philippines (1972)	78%	Colombia	66%
Sri Lanka (1970)	77%	Mexico	60%
Bangladesh (1973)	75%	Costa Rica	55%
		India	53%

Source: Sinha, 1984

Even with the initiation of agrarian reforms, the politics of land ownership often work to ensure that the most productive land remains in the hands of a few. Where political power resides with a land-owning elite, governments allow private estates to expand further and protect their boundaries. In Colombia, land reform has meant the modernization and capitalization of existing estates, leading to even greater concentration of ownership (Leon de Leal, 1985). In El Salvador, the land reform of 1980 brought no significant change in the plight of the country's 2.5 million landless or near-landless peasants (Pearce, 1986). Here, as in many Third World countries, the poorest are squeezed on to marginal lands which are steep, infertile, dry, subject to pests or disease or covered with rainforest. Their attempts to grow subsistence crops result only in increased erosion and the destruction of water and fuelwood resources. Where many people are forced on to poor land, fallow periods diminish or disappear and the possibilities for soil recovery are reduced. Scarce energy sources cause people to burn

4

manure and crop residues to meet their fuel needs, and the loss of these traditional sources of soil nutrients decreases land fertility. It is estimated that the annual burning of 400 million tonnes of dung depresses the world's grain harvest by over fourteen million tonnes (Spears, 1978).

Women produce food

Many of those dispossessed of land by the increasing concentration of ownership are women and their children. Women have title to only 1 per cent of the world's land. Yet they produce more than half of the world's food – and in countries of food scarcity the percentage is even higher. Women produce more than 80 per cent of the food for Sub-Saharan Africa, 50-60 per cent of Asia's food, 46 per cent in the Caribbean, 31 per cent in North Africa and the Middle East and more than 30 per cent in Latin America (FAO 1986; Foster, 1986.

Figure 2: *Percentage of total agricultural production by women*

Nepal	98%	Iraq	41%
Zaire	64%	Brazil	32%
Korea	51%	Colombia	20%

Source: Jiggins, 1984

Women make up the majority of subsistence farmers. In most rural cultures, it is their work which provides a family with its basic diet and with any supplementary food that may be obtained from barter or from selling surplus goods. Underestimating the amount of agricultural work done by women is very common, for statistics most often measure wage labour, not unpaid kitchen-garden work. Moreover, in some cultures men do not wish to admit that their wives, mothers and daughters do agricultural work. For these reasons, the vital contribution that women make to food production is consistently under represented (Taylor *et al.*, 1985).

Women also participate actively in cash-crop production, either as extra hands at harvest time or as employees on large farms. Women can sometimes spend more time in export production than men. In Nigeria, for example, women work more than men

5

in the cocoa plantations, in coffee production for export, and in national market crops such as rice, grain, maize and cassava (Fresco, 1985). In Nicaragua in 1980, women made up 28 per cent of coffee harvesters and 32 per cent of cotton workers (IFDP, 1980).

MORE TECHNOLOGY, LESS SOIL FERTILITY

Increasing agricultural industrialization, particularly under the "Green Revolution" introduced in the 1950s, has had an enormous effect on women. This policy of intensifying food production through developing hybrid, high-yield seed varieties demanded extensive irrigation and increased mechanization, as well as the use of fertilizers and pesticides. Chemical and biological technology was applied on a large scale in South-East Asia, India, China and Mexico, with the goal of increasing food production. Yields did increase, often dramatically. Between 1974 and 1983 they grew at more than 2 per cent each year – largely as a result of the increased productivity of land already under cultivation. But in spite of this increase the people of South-East Asia and India are still among the least well-nourished in the world. The Green Revolution has produced no increase in *per capita* food consumption and has in many cases reduced it (Lappé and Collins, 1986). Instead, the Green Revolution has contributed to erosion, desertification, and greater concentrations of land-ownership, removing land from those most in need.

Erosion and desertification are not merely a result of rainfall:

> Only appropriate land use can keep arid zones ecologically stable and biologically productive. Inappropriate land use can destabilize even humid regions, undermining biological productivity and causing desertification. Since the large majority of people in countries like India have livelihoods based on on land, the long-term decline of the biological productivity of land undermines livelihoods and results in underdevelopment. (Bandyopadhyay and Shiva, 1986:1)

Large scale, mechanized, highly technological agriculture is extremely taxing on land fertility. Widespread irrigation – probably the most effective way to increase yields – can cause waterlogging, a reduction of essential minerals, and salinization because of increased evaporation. More than a third of all land under irrigation is subject to salinization, alkalinization and waterlogging (UNEP, 1980). In some areas, 80 per cent of the irrigated land has been destroyed in these ways. Worldwide, salinization alone may require the abandonment of as much land as is now under irrigation (World Resources, 1986).

Synthetic petroleum-based fertilizers are also the cause of serious soil and water pollution. Experiments show that this kind of agriculture affects the metabolic balance in plants, leaving them more vulnerable to attack from pests and diseases. Farmers are then caught in the vicious circle of increasingly intensive (and costly) use of pesticides, which in turn causes greater pest infestation (Guazzelli, 1985). There is growing concern over the developing immunity of many pest species as pesticide use accelerates, especially in developing countries.

Pesticide use also has serious consequences for health. During informal consultations in 1985, the World Health Organization estimated that one million cases of pesticide poisoning occur annually. Not only human beings, but many other non-target species (and livelihoods based on them) are affected by pesticide poisoning, including livestock, fish, birds and bees (Bull, 1982).

The introduction of laboratory-bred hybrid crop species has also had negative consequences. In the district of Dharwar, India, for example, a mix of indigenous varieties of crops were cultivated, giving high yields of fodder, pulses and oilseeds. These varieties were drought-resistant and, in normal rainfall years, produced food that could be stored for the drought years. The introduction of a single hybrid Jower (sorghum) not only reduced fodder production, but also made the crop susceptible to failure in short drought periods because of a decrease in absorbent organic matter being added to the soil (Bandyopadhyay and Shiva, 1986).

Promoting the use of hybrid seeds also diminishes the genetic resource base of many crops, leaving farmers dependent on fewer, perhaps less adaptable, varieties in the face of changing weather conditions. A Sri Lankan farmer remembered 123 varieties of red rice; now only four remain. He has one acre of paddy which, in a very good year, produces 100 bushels of rice – a surplus of 25 bushels. But, because each of the traditional varieties was less vulnerable to severe conditions than the hybrid variety now in use and because the hybrid does not keep long in storage, he requires an ever-increasing surplus on which to live (ICDA, 1985). In this way, new technology has reduced farmers' self-reliance.

The pressure to engage in industrialized agriculture has increased with the changing global pattern of food trade. Many developed countries depend for their food supply on land use in developing countries. United States hamburgers are increasingly made from the beef produced on cattle ranches in Latin America. Extensive ranching, which has reached into the Amazon basin, is now destroying a reservoir of plant and animal species of great genetic diversity (Lappé, Collins and Fowler, 1978). Recent studies have also shown that Dutch agriculture uses a land area in the Third World five times the size of its own cultivated land to supply the cattle fodder and raw materials for food products (Netherlands, 1986).

Patterns of agriculture that demand enormous economic and chemical inputs do nothing to ameliorate critical food shortages. Instead, they increase these shortages through dependence on an economic and industrial order which excludes the very people who are most in need.

More work for women

All of these consequences of industrialized agriculture impinge upon the everyday lives of women attempting to glean food, fuel and water from their environment. Many effects are confined to women because of the gender-specific division of labour in rural agricultural societies. In most cultures, women are responsible for food processing, fuel and water gathering. "In the agricultural sector of Africa, women perform 80 per cent of the storing, 90 per cent of food processing, 60 per cent of the marketing and 50 per cent of the domestic animal care . . . often with few, if any, modern tools" (ILO/INSTRAW, 1985). However, specific tasks allocated by gender are renegotiated in response to changing conditions – in ecological conditions, in social structures, and in economic relations, among many others (Creevey, 1986). Thus women's agricultural work – in fields, weeding, harvesting, irrigating, tending poultry and small grazing animals or cattle, food preparation and marketing – depends on where they live and their place in the rural economy (ISIS, 1983). For example, husbandry of livestock is often women's work, but what that actually means will vary. In Pakistan, women care for small livestock and cattle. In Chile, 80 per cent of the small-scale women farmers also tend livestock. Up to 90 per cent of rural women in North Africa, Asia and Latin America keep poultry, and in several Sahelian countries women are the major goat-tenders. Whether this responsibility includes carrying water, gathering fodder, securing animals from predators, preparing for market or marketing will be different in each country.

The spread of erosion and desertification makes all of these tasks more difficult or even impossible. As women's contribution to their own well-being becomes more problematic, their marginalization increases. When access to fertile land diminishes – as intensive agriculture eats up the small plots of the poor – women are displaced to more distant, fragile and less fertile lands, or even become landless labourers. Without land, women have no access to credit, training or other aids to production.

The number of landless people worldwide is growing dramatically (UNEP, 1980). In Pakistan, India and Bangladesh, one-quarter of the population has no land, and this group is growing fast. The majority of the landless are women. Where efforts are made to address the problem of landlessness, as with land reform, the situation of women is exacerbated: women's traditional and existing land rights do not figure in the calculation as to how to reallocate land (Foster, 1986).

With the displacement of subsistence agriculture to less fertile areas, women who still have access to land must travel longer distances to their fields. When they arrive, they must work harder to compensate for severe erosion and low fertility. When their plots are exhausted, they must wander elsewhere in search of food. In the Ivory Coast, women have had to leave their own fields because of expanding agroindustrial coconut and palm oil plantations. They were forced to move into the Tai Forest, where farming not only caused environmental damage, but the land they used was not suitable for permanent agriculture (Bamba, 1985). Environmental degradation of this kind has other consequences as well. In Mozambique, not only political instability but erosion and environmental degradation are causing increasing numbers of refugees to move into Zimbabwe, imposing extra burdens on the capacity of Zimbabwean resources.

The "double" day

As the transition to cash-cropping makes inroads on rural agriculture, women's activities become both more burdensome and less socially valued. Marginalization occurs where there is a desperate and pervasive demand for cash to meet family needs. If those needs can be supplied only by the market, unpaid traditional roles will no longer evoke respect, thereby undercutting the authority of women (Huston, 1985). Women's subsistence agriculture suffers from neglect where large-scale agriculture absorbs labour, land and economic resources. At the same time the labour necessary for survival increases. In Cameroon, for example, men were given land, water, seeds and technical training to enable them to produce rice for sale. Women were then expected to carry out their traditional agricultural tasks in the cash-crop rice fields, as well as cultivating sorghum for their families (Foster, 1986). This pattern in women's lives, called "the double day", has been a perennial accompaniment to transitions from rural to industrial capitalist economies. And the work that women are expected to do in growing cash crops – planting and weeding – is often more gruelling than men's work, for men generally run the farm machinery. The increase in yields that follows the use of fertilizers, pesticides, high-yield seed varieties and mechanization can mean more work for women. In Sierra Leone the introduction of tractors and modern ploughs resulted in a decrease of the working day for men in the rice culture, but women had to work 50 per cent more to finish weeding and maintaining the larger fields.

The use of pesticides can also displace women. In Kenya and Uganda, the widespread use of insecticides and fungicides has made many women, who formerly did 85 per cent of the weeding by hand, redundant (Morse, 1978). And finally, because large-scale agriculture attracts migrants from other areas in search of work, it increases the competition for jobs.

These changes have meant that the proportion of women among farmers in India has decreased from 45 per cent in 1951 to 30 per cent in 1971, while the participation of female labourers rose from 31 to 51 per cent over the same period (after the introduction of the Green Revolution). For these women, the high-yielding rice technology may have increased employment opportunities, but particularly for women of poorer households, the result was also an increased workload without any improvement in their standard of living (Agarwal, 1986).

In other ways, too, large-scale industrialized agriculture affects women for the worse. Intensive fertilizer use, for example, requires a great deal of water, but in many countries there is no surplus. In Zimbabwe and India the water table is steadily falling as a result of irrigation and fertilizer use. This may also contaminate local water supplies. In Zimbabwe, women who were used to collecting drinking water from wells in the fields where they worked can no longer do so because the well water is contaminated by fertilizers used on the land (Nyoni, 1985). And in Haiti, women use the water from the irrigation ditches since they do not have access to a source free of chemical runoff (personal communication, Susan Quinlan, IFDP, 1986). Thus where once women could fulfil their family needs for water locally, they now must travel several kilometres or use contaminated sources.

In the state of Rajasthan, India, now on the brink of a desertification disaster, wells and once-flowing rivers are dry. In 1975, the World Bank and its partners introduced capital-intensive irrigated farming in that area. A region of just 60 centimetres of rainfall a year was planted with sugar cane, which has such a high water requirement that groundwater levels have fallen dramatically. Crops fail and people starve (Shiva, 1985b).

As food providers, women play a central role in the nutritional intake of the family. But this is similarly affected by the development of large-scale monocultures producing crops for export at the expense of subsistence foods. The complementary structure of rural diet – beans and corn or lentils and rice, for example – has been undermined not only by these shifts but also by intensive marketing of commercially processed products such as Coca-Cola and bread (Lappé and Collins, 1978; ISIS, 1983). Agricultural change linked to glistening images of progress alters nutritional intake, and makes women's task of feeding the family that much more difficult. Health suffers and malnutrition increases.

Finally, large-scale agricultural expansion places impossible demands on women, who may have access to land but rarely to the capital or credit to invest in machinery, hybrid seeds or chemicals. The inputs required by Green Revolution agriculture are usually beyond their economic reach. "When you cannot afford to drink the milk from your own buffalo, but must sell it to buy wheat, what possibility is there of purchasing fertilizers and imported seeds?" (Taylor *et al.*, 1985). In some villages in India, women have pawned their silver jewellery, their only property, to meet the costs of new seeds, fertilizers and pesticides, thereby removing any economic independence they might have had (Shiva, 1985a). But for most women who must work all day in the fields raising wheat or cassava, any investment in agricultural machinery is far beyond their reach, culturally as well as financially (Whitehead, 1985). To an Indian woman whose wages may be controlled by her husband and who must sit on the floor while he sits on the only chair, owning or even driving a tractor is inconceivable. And yet some development projects are blind to these circumstances, assuming that the only difficulty for women is a lack of funds. Because of the centrality of women's labour to rural survival, lack of attention to the particular effects that the development of industrial agriculture has had on women is especially damaging. The responsibilities and skills of rural women in fulfilling their families' food, fuel and water needs must be accorded their full economic and social significance if development efforts are to be of real assistance to Third World people.

WOMEN LOSE THEIR RIGHTS

Most developing countries have a long history of colonial rule which imposed laws and social structures particularly harmful to women. Among these are inheritance laws, legislation on land-ownership and transfer, and social restrictions on women which seriously limit their activities and aspirations.

These patterns have occurred extensively in Africa, but European laws and customs have also altered the place of women in Central America so as to reduce their power. Inheritance laws and communal rights to land which once allowed access by women have been replaced by title-deed systems which, by law or custom, restrict land-ownership to individual men (Jiggins, 1984; Poldermans, 1985). Spanish colonization in Latin America brought with it an ideology of chastity and dependence which has dominated women's lives in Africa, where market organization of women traders once allowed women political and economic power, and where sister/brother inheritance and kin co-operation patterns allowed women an alternative to dependence on a husband, European patriarchy undermined both (Sachs, 1982).

Men migrate

These same developments, especially since the Second World War, have fostered the growth of industrial centres which draw men away from rural communities, removing their labour from subsistence farming. The increasing migration of men to the cities, to mines, to export agriculture, or to work abroad has caused the number of female-headed households to rise dramatically. This often means that the entire responsibility for feeding, clothing and housing children rests on the woman's shoulders. Recent studies of seventy-four developing countries show that women already head more than a fifth of the households in Africa and the Caribbean, and 15 per cent of those in Latin America, the Middle East and North Africa. For some countries, the figures are much higher: in Kenya, Botswana, Ghana and Sierra Leone almost half the households are headed by women (Taylor et al., 1985). In Lesotho they are called "widows of the gold", as their husbands migrate seasonally to South Africa to work in the mines, where eight thousand have died in the past decade. A US Agency for International Development (USAID) study shows that female-headed households are the poorest group in every country (Foster, 1986).

Discrimination in wages and training

When rural women do participate in the wage-labour economy, they face discrimination and lower wage rates. In countries which are trying to meet rural needs through the development of agroindustry, discrimination in job classification and wages is especially intense. Helen Safa reports that 70 per cent of jobs in food processing for export are women's jobs, because they can be paid at much lower rates. In countries like Mexico, which has the highest investment in food processing of any country in the world, agroindustrial development is seen as a solution to rural poverty. In these industries the lowest-paid jobs are reserved for women. Strawberry-processing plants in Zamora employ 10,000 young rural women to stem strawberries, select and pack them at wages well below the legal minimum (Arizipe and Aranda, 1986). In the Philippines, women working on sugar haciendas earn 2-3 pesos to men's 4-5 (Eviota, 1986). More than half of the working women in Java, Indonesia earn less than 3,000 rupiahs per year, while only 14 per cent of the men earn so little (Taylor *et al.*, 1985).

Where women remain in subsistence agriculture their central position is usually ignored, even by development professionals. Thus training and agricultural extension programmes often fail to reach women. Out of a study of forty-six African countries it became clear that less than 4 per cent of extension workers who advise women are themselves women. In Asia, the proportion is 7 per cent. The impact of even this small percentage is greater than it appears, because in Muslim cultures it is prohibited for women to be taught by a man (FAO, 1984). In some Hindu and Christian cultures, too, customs preclude an open learning atmosphere between women and a male non-family member.

But this is not the sole problem. The teaching of non-middle-class women is not even considered in many areas. "Women have not been part of the mainstream of educational activity anywhere in the developing world" (ISIS, 1983: 176). Yet illiterate women, out of reach of extension workers, are especially vulnerable to the injudicious use of dangerous chemicals. Spraying of fields and local storage of unsafe chemicals are special hazards for these women, whose children also suffer if their mothers are poisoned during pregnancy (Dankelman, 1985). In Central America, more and more women are found with poisoned milk from pesticides. Such consequences for women and children are wholly overlooked when the focus of attention in evaluating development is narrowed to the amount that yields have increased.

All of these unplanned effects of development – development that can be described as "gender-blind" – have led to increasingly desperate circumstances for women and their families. In Brazil, for example, they leave the countryside for the large cities, but the limited options for work there have intensified their poverty. Many women must work in the "informal" sector, selling food and other goods on the streets or doing domestic work. Others are forced into prostitution. And high rates of delinquency are observed among children (Guazzelli, 1985).

Listen to the women

Gender-blind development has another consequence: it undermines ecologically sound traditional agricultural knowledge. It should be clear that women, as the world's most important food producers, are directly dependent on a healthy environment. It is also becoming more and more obvious how much rural women themselves are conscious of this dependence and how much they know about their natural environment, soil conditions and crops. As a rural woman from Zimbabwe said: "My environment is the basis of my economy and my total survival. It is from the land that I get my food" (Nyoni, 1985).

Women's agricultural methods, practised successfully for over forty centuries in countries like India and China, adapt to the environment and are sustainable without long-term damage to the land (Shiva, 1985a). The knowledge and experience of generations permit women to have great flexibility in cropping practices. For example, the serious decline in soil fertility in many parts of Africa has caused them to shift their cropping from maize to cassava. Although the traditionally used cassava root offers less nutritional value than maize, women have begun to use all parts of the plant, including its leaves, in meal preparation so that there is actually an increased intake of calories and proteins (Fresco, 1985).

Women's agricultural knowledge provides security for themselves and for others. As long as women are still engaged in seed selection, the future survival of traditional crops is assured. In Zimbabwe, a woman too poor to purchase new millet seeds used traditional ones. Later droughts caused others' harvests to fail, but her crop survived. A women's organization purchased twenty-five bags of her traditional seeds and distributed them to other women throughout many villages (van Brakel, 1986).

Today's hybrid varieties do not reproduce fertile seeds; the farmer must buy new seed every year. She is now completely at the mercy of the seed-supply system. Over time, she may lose her traditional knowledge of seeds since she no longer selects them after each harvest for the following year. Modern agricultural practices thus contribute to the genetic erosion of crop varieties, and women become more dependent on the purchase of hybrid seeds.

Women know that participating in the new agricultural technology threatens their only means of control over their livelihoods: "In Tanzania, when new hybrid maize seeds, fertilizer and pesticides were allotted to men by the government, the women who do most of the field work neglected the new crop. Although their workload with the old crop was heavier, the profits from the new crop would, by tradition, have gone only to men" (*WorldWIDE News*, 1986 (1):4). In Ghana, rural women were reluctant to accept new hybrid maize seeds since the crop had an unpleasant taste, was hard to prepare, was less resistant to drought and insects, required different storage methods and depended on chemical fertilizers which changed the taste. Although these objections were rational they were not considered by the development agency (Ahmed, 1985).

But the belief that women's knowledge cannot be scientific has kept it from being recognized and threatened its survival. In tribal Indian villages, women were growing high-yielding, indigenous varieties of rice, but because the women were considered backward and not scientific enough, "modern" agriculture was introduced (Shiva, 1985a). There are, moreover, economic pressures against building on traditional knowledge – for those who profit by selling the prerequisites of industrial agriculture want to do so frequently. Indigenous methods do not require financial investment at every planting.

WAYS FORWARD

Because of this [food] crisis, we are interested in sustainable agriculture, not for luxury, not for economic reasons, but first and foremost for our own survival (Nyoni, 1985:53).

Sustainable agriculture is food production which respects both the natural and social environment. It is based on wise use of natural and renewable resources with moderate exploitation (Shiva, 1985a). And sustainable agriculture is controlled by the community it supports, so that it may flexibly respond to the needs both of people and their environment.

In practice, sustainable agriculture requires:

- equitable access by all farmers to fertile lands, credit and agricultural information;
- the maintenance and support of independent agriculture over which rural farmers, both women and men, have control themselves;
- the development of cultivation, food processing and food storage methods which ease the intense demands on women's labour;
- a high degree of species diversification to maintain flexible cropping patterns;
- the conservation of fertile soils in which organic matter is recycled (to avoid dependence on imported nutrients); and
- an appropriate use of water and fuel resources.

A variety of methods is now in use to conserve land resources and the diversity of species. New styles of landscape planning encourage a diversity of habitats, integrating trees with crops. Mulching, multiple cropping and crop rotation, the use of compost and green manure, can all improve soil fertility along with the integration of animal husbandry, use of natural fertilizers, special varieties and pioneer plants for soils. Selective weeding and integrated pest control have improved crop protection. These methods have produced higher yields over a longer period and reduced the dependency on expensive external inputs. Furthermore, they allow agriculturists to maintain a healthy environment. They incorporate traditional knowledge and expertise, particularly of the woman farmer, increasing her self-reliance and her control over the process of agricultural production. Although these management methods for sustainable agriculture will not remove the injustices of land distribution or other inequalities and discriminations that characterize global patterns of food production, they are a start.

Locally, groups of women in diverse communities have been working towards wider goals. In Zimbabwe, women are demanding land-ownership as well as participation in co-operatives (Weiss, 1986). In Nicaragua, where hard-won land reform makes access to land legally possible for women, the national women's organization is working for social changes that will improve this access, and has negotiated with unions for day-care facilities in agricultural areas (Davies, 1983). And Carmen Diana Deere reports that women in Nicaragua have pushed for communal eating areas at rural work centres, thus mitigating the "double day" (*Feminist Theory*, 49). In the Dominican Republic, local women's groups spread techniques of intensive small-scale gardening which were both agriculturally self-sustaining and soil-conserving on overlogged hillsides (Chaney, 1985). By January 1983, there were 6,000 of these household gardens in the Dominican Republic (Nash and Safa, 1986).

The Wum Area Oxen Project, begun in 1976 by the Cameroon government and the West German Agency for Technical Co-operation, is now transforming women's lives in the mountainous north west of Cameroon. The use of oxen for ploughing, harrowing, raking, mulching and transport has replaced backbreaking hand cultivation, which previously took from dawn to dark, and required leaving children unattended and household chores undone. The project offers farmers a two-month training course in the use and maintenance of draught animals. Preference is given to women's groups which can send at least four members to be trained; there are now thirty-four groups participating. At the start of the training session, every farmer or group is given a pair of oxen.

The use of oxen has increased the land under cultivation, and increased the number of crops harvested in a year. In many areas wheat, rice and soya beans are now planted in addition to the traditional groundnuts and maize. Bananas, plantains, cassava and yams are also grown and rotated with fodder crops and legumes to maintain soil fertility. Mixed farming can thus make even a small farm viable, and help ensure adequate long-term food supply (Barry, 1986).

Women in Gambia have embarked on a soil-preservation scheme by building dykes which prevent salt water from encroaching on their rice fields. The Gambian National Women's Bureau has also introduced orchard woodlots managed by village women's groups. These will bring firewood closer to home as well as improve nutrition by supplying families with fruits and vegetables. Women are planting nursery bed and spice plots as well. These practices enrich the soil, prevent erosion, increase crop diversity and provide fuel and shade.

In Rajasthan, India, where, as discussed earlier, large-scale sugar cane production has undermined local agriculture, women have been the driving force behind the Chipko movement. Acting against the advice of the Forestry Research Institute, women planted oak trees in deforested regions, so providing a new basis for water, fodder and fertilizer (Shiva, 1985b). Elsewhere in India, the Self-Employed Women's Association (SEWA) of Ahmedabad has sponsored cattle and dairy projects for landless agricultural labourers. These women were paid not in cash, but in food grains or fodder; the switch to self-employment, and the development of dairies, milk co-operatives and a subsidized cattle-feed programme have given them income and independence. SEWA members now run the milk business themselves: they tend the cattle, sell the milk and deal with the banks and moneylenders. Says one observer: "SEWA is not just an office or an organization, it is a women's movement. It is definitely making a dent in the policies for poor women and their self-image" (Braun, 1984).

The following case studies describe some pioneering examples of sustainable agriculture from Africa, Latin America and the Middle East. They are a small sample of what can be done to improve the circumstances of women in agriculture. The International Fund for Agricultural Development (IFAD) and the UN Fund for Women (UNIFEM) are among the United Nations agencies which support these efforts. But much more remains to be done. Efforts will succeed only where the needs and desires of women, as well as the overwhelming responsibilities facing them, become the starting points for action. If underdevelopment is to be addressed, the farmer herself must be recognized and empowered. Enabling rural women to change their lives will require a restructuring of social and political controls over agriculture and land so that a woman may participate in the decisions affecting her life. This will be a long process, but progress toward this goal is not impossible, as the examples show. Development agencies, women's organizations and rural grass roots groups of all kinds must continue to use their energy and imagination to reclaim an agriculture that will sustain women, their families and the environment for years to come.

CASE STUDIES

WOMEN AND SOYA BEANS IN TOGO, WEST AFRICA

According to Togolese tradition, women prepare the special condiment dawa dawa mustard sauce. Dawa dawa seeds are scarce and expensive; they take time to gather and require lengthy preparation. Deforestation in Togo has reduced an already limited supply of the trees from which the seed is collected and from which the wood, needed to boil the sauce for twenty-four hours, is gathered. The need to find an alternative to the dawa dawa seed has triggered a valuable development project for women.

In Togo, as in most other parts of Africa, women are responsible for feeding their families. Men provide the staple grains of sorghum or millet; women supply the vegetables, seasonings, meat and sauces. All are costly. The result is a frighteningly high level of malnutrition among Togolese children – up to 60 per cent in some villages during the "lean season". Both development and nutrition educational programmes have failed to solve the problem. Food aid is available through some local clinics, but it is often not suited to local tastes or physiology.

Since 1979, World Neighbours has collaborated with Family

Health Advisory Services (FHAS) in Togo to help women look for resources near to hand as solutions to their problems. This approach has enabled them to make use of not only local crops but also their own skills in working co-operatively.

The soya bean project
A major success has been the introduction of soya beans, a relatively new crop to West Africa but one which has become the entry point for an integrated programme of farming and family health in the three countries of Togo, Ghana and Mali. Soya beans are an ideal crop for poor women: they improve both nutrition and the environment. With a 40 per cent protein content, these legumes fix nitrogen from the air and produce good yields without fertilizer – often double the yield of local beans. Soya beans grow fast and resist drought and many of the insect pests and parasites common in tropical West Africa. Apart from seed, no inputs are needed.

Soya bean cultivation has been tried here before and failed. What is different now is the approach of Ayele Foly and Alice Iddi, the two West African leaders of FHAS. They looked first at women's immediate needs and then developed the project by helping the women to test a new idea on a small scale, encouraging them, and training local women to train others.

Even before the FHAS project, a few women were cultivating local soya bean varieties; FHAS began to promote what these women had learnt. The crop was first introduced as a legume that could be used to make sauces, not as a commercial crop in which men would have an interest. The men did not, therefore, resist when the women asked for small plots of land to grow the beans. FHAS recruited and trained a small number of volunteers to cultivate the crop on trial plots and to share their success with others. It then organized cooking demonstrations, showing women how to prepare their local dishes with soya beans, and getting them to compare the results with food cooked using their usual ingredients. Slides were shown of other villages where soya beans were used; exchange visits were arranged between soya-bean- and non-soya-bean-growing villages. These exchange visits and the workshops in women's homes have proved to be highly popular and have provided, FHAS argues, a more effective training environment than an unfamiliar urban study centre. The pioneers return from these workshops to their own villages, where they train other women to grow and use the soya beans. The process makes good use of women's natural leadership qualities and their willingness and ability to work together, and moves the project towards its long-term goal – to strengthen the status and economic position of Togolese women.

The key to gaining widespread acceptance of the new crop was the promotion of soya beans as a substitute for the seed bean used to make dawa dawa mustard, the highly prized ingredient of most local sauces. Later, women began to use the soya bean in other dishes and to make a high-protein porridge for their children. FHAS helped mothers to identify malnourished children (by coloured armbands), and trained some of the women as volunteer health workers.

Benefits
In Togo, Ghana and Mali, more than a thousand women now cultivate soya beans as a result of the FHAS programme. Malnutrition among children has been significantly reduced. The projects have enabled women to generate an income for their families by selling surplus soya beans (raw or as flour or mustard) in local markets. They are saving money previously spent on imported flavourings or dawa dawa seeds. Now, women participate more fully in family decision-making – especially about the use of land.

Source: Peter Gubbels and Alice Iddi, 1986.

THE PINABETAL WOMEN'S ORGANIZATION, MEXICO
Living in the mountains to the south of the town of San Cristóbal de las Casas, Chiapas, are small communities of Indian peasant families, the Tzotzil. They have been there since the big landholdings and plantations ceased to be productive – a direct result of the overuse of land and the gradual transformation of feudal farms into agribusinesses. In the arid, stony areas which overlook the fertile valleys of the Grijalva River in central Chiapas, these families, and the women especially, are fighting the poverty which surrounds them.

There is a strong collective tradition in these communities. They have installed water points and electricity supplies, and built schools. But for women the story was familiar. However crucial they were to the success of the projects, women were allowed no part in the structure or decision-making of local organizations. The activities which directly concerned them, such as the rearing of small animals, were not given priority in the male-dominated co-operatives of most of the communities. Nor could women get loans to improve their economic position: there was consistent discrimination against them in the use of a local revolving loan fund.

In 1981, a group of women based in Pinabetal formed a collective to overcome this discrimination and to tackle some of the major problems the women face – lack of access to land, no roads, no schools, no work. After years of struggle, the Pinebetal Women's Organization has succeeded in buying land for the women to cultivate together.

The Pinabetal Organization now involves thirty peasant women. They work collectively to grow vegetables, raise sheep for wool and as a source of natural fertilizer, and are planning to keep dairy cattle to provide milk. Current projects, in part supported by OXFAM, include chicken-rearing, water management, more vegetable plots and soil-conservation measures.

Important as these achievements are, they are not the final answer. The Tzotzil women need to lift themselves out of their extreme poverty, but to accomplish this in the long run they need confidence, skills and experience. Fore this reason, the Pinebetal Organization runs study groups and evaluation and planning sessions, in which its members decide the shape and priorities of their collective. As Indian women, they also benefit from discussion about the situation of indigenous women farmers. The women of the Pinabetal Women's Organization now hope that their success will be replicated in neighbouring villages, where women want to find ways of working together to solve their problems.

Source: OXFAM. UK

THE VACARIA PROJECT IN BRAZIL
Since the 1960s, Brazilian agricultural policy has emphasized Green Revolution technology as a model of production and development.

That model, based on expensive foreign inputs (chemical fertilizers and pesticides, heavy machinery and hybrid seeds), has been promoted through subsidized bank credits. Production is characterized by monoculture and this has destroyed the peasant social structure in southern Brazil. Increasing impoverishment of the land is driving farmers into the Amazonian rainforests of northern Brazil and to the urban centres. In order to achieve social changes that would relieve the situation, Ação Democrática Feminina Gaúcha (ADFG), the Friends of the Earth in Brazil, is implementing a combined environment and development project co-ordinated by women.

With financial support from Friends of the Earth in Sweden, and the Swedish International Development Authority, a project on Low External Input Agriculture was begun in February 1985. The project involves the management of a farm and a training centre, with a programme for peasants, extension workers and students from agronomy and veterinary faculties. The administrative and technical co-ordinator for agricultural matters is a woman agriculturalist, while a woman veterinary surgeon co-ordinates animal-related matters.

The farm is located at Vacaria in the highlands of southern Brazil. Its 50 hectares (of which 25 are natural woodland) are managed to include cropping, gardening, fruit-growing, animal husbandry and agroforestry. The main goal of the project is to demonstrate that sustainable agriculture can make small farms viable, providing work for unskilled labour and slowing migration to the cities and rainforests. It is hoped that the demonstration will bring about changes in Brazil's agricultural policy.

Sustainable agriculture is based on the adoption of techniques that increase soil fertility or maintain fertility indefinitely. The approach aims to protect the environment, keep the energy balance, and to control erosion without using chemical fertilizers and pesticides and by integrating a diversity of crops and animal production. Most of the inputs are locally or regionally produced so that food production is freed from international arrangements and trends that create dependency. The technology is also less expensive than modern technology – a distinct advantage in view of Brazil's current economic crisis.

At its inception, the ADFG project gained widespread support. But it was also strongly criticized: in addition to launching a new agricultural concept in opposition to large corporate pressure, two young women were running a project in a traditionally male domain. Since then, however, results have been so successful that people from many different backgrounds – students, church extension workers, peasants and farmers – have requested advice and training. Around the project area, a reduction in land exploitation is already noticeable as farmers have begun to use the sustainable agriculture techniques pioneered by the Vacaria project.

Source: Maria José Guazzelli, ADFG.

TRIBAL WOMEN IN IRAN

In 1974, a pilot project on rural development was started in the mountainous region of Lorestan in the east of Iran. The local population, most of which was recently nomadic, numbers 35,000. The main objective was to promote sustainable development of natural resources through the use of appropriate technologies. It was hoped that external dependence, a dominant characteristic of underdevelopment, would gradually be eliminated.

A second objective was to help the women of that recently settled society to reclaim the important role they had played in the nomadic society of their past – without destroying the family nucleus. In contrast to their role in sedentary agricultural societies, women in nomadic communities play an active part in making decisions. Some of these societies could even be called matriarchal.

The project began by selecting extension workers, particularly women, from the local population. The workers were divided into four units: hygiene and health, agriculture, education, and rural industries and domestic economies. Health was a top priority: sixteen extension workers – half the total group – were responsible for women and children's health and family planning.

The agricultural unit aimed to promote sustainable development through the use of scientifically appropriate cultivation and animal husbandry methods. The unit also tackled the reduction of malaria mosquitos by relocating the habitat of the larvae, by improving human and animal hygiene and by introducing suitable irrigation techniques. In their nomadic past, the population had used the moulded dung of cows as domestic fuel; it was now necessary to find an alternative. The agricultural unit installed a biogas plant which met several goals: energy supply, environmental care and, most important, the recycling of organic wastes to the land.

The rural industries and domestic economies unit was formed exclusively of women. They decided to increase family living standards by promoting the weaving of handicrafts, using the traditional motifs and natural dye and methods which had been lost after settlement. The products are now a commercial success, as is the small-scale production of educational indigenous toys, which met almost all the needs of the 300 to 400 children in the district.

The Lorestan project has succeeded. Women in the health unit play an important role in family planning, disease prevention and simple healing. The education unit pioneered innovative literacy techniques and the use of a curriculum based on local culture. Women's living standards were raised as the rural industries and domestic economies group started to make and market products. Only in the agriculture unit did the presence of women extension workers create friction: men thought that it was abnormal for the four women to drive tractors, work the land, help build the biogas plant and treat animals. But, along with the measurable improvements in agriculture, the unit showed that women could take effective responsibility in agricultural affairs and animal husbandry.

Their success shows how easy it is, with a small effort, to give women confidence and to raise their awareness of their capabilities. Today the women of the region work outside the home without problems and possess a craft skill. Twelve years after the start of the project – twelve years of revolution and war – there is a noticeable difference between the women in the project area and those in neighbouring regions.

Fundamental to the success of the experiment has been its method of dialogue between project officers, extension workers and the people. At the end of each week, extension workers went home and discussed the issues with the people in their villages; they returned with many new ideas. This method requires a certain level of awareness among peasants and development workers, and sensitivity on the part of the researchers themselves. The principal goal has been to change hierarchical relationships into horizontal ones, and to formulate needs as objectives, classified in order of priority. The people were encouraged to determine their own future.

Foreign extension workers were replaced by indigenous specialists, and the freedom to speak openly and to criticize was protected.

The political situation in Iran still does not encourage group discussions about solving rural problems, but the project has had a major impact. Women in the area are now openly discussing politics, their own emancipation and their political opinions with outsiders. The same women, in 1974 when the project began, would not have met foreigners nor, even if they had political opinions, would they have been able to express them.

Source: Khadijek Catherine Razavi Farvar, Rural Development Associate, Centre for Ecodevelopment Studies and Application, Tehran, Iran.

HORTICULTURE IN GOLGOTTA SETTLEMENT, ETHIOPIA

For many years, the Ethiopian countryside was decimated by a growing number of peasants applying "slash and burn" methods of cultivation. Together with constant forest fires, "slash and burn" stripped the environment of its vegetation. Adverse climatic conditions in the lowlands forced 85 per cent of the population to move up into the highlands. The country was exposed to repeated drought and famine.

In 1974, the Relief and Rehabilitation Commission (RRC) was created to co-ordinate efforts to repair the environmental devastation, and to initiate a programme of rehabilitation and preventive action in a number of new refugee settlements. For women, the programme was pretty much a failure. For one thing, the dependent status of most women worked against their full participation in RRC programmes – a social reality that was overlooked by the organization. For another, the structure of the settlement programmes excluded many women: only widows and women deserted by their husbands qualified for "settler status".

The Golgotta Settlement Horticultural Initiative grew out of the concern that women refugees were not taking part in the RRC development projects. The Revolutionary Ethiopian Women's Association (REWA), founded in 1981 and backed by women's groups and the FAO's Freedom from Hunger Campaign Action for Development, was given the go-ahead to start a pilot project.

After assessing women's needs, REWA decided on horticulture: this would obviously provide them with food, and the fact that women would be working together would help alleviate the loneliness and insecurity of life in a settlement camp.

Golgotta, a settlement 180 kilometres from Addis Ababa, was chosen as the project site. REWA was allocated five hectares in one of the Golgotta camps with easy access to water, and promised another ten hectares if the project succeeded. RRC provided the training for both settlers and project staff.

A hundred women were involved. They began to plant immediately – watermelon, red beet and carrots – covering just over half the allotted area. In their second venture, the women planted onions, peppers and tomatoes. Harvests were good and the produce was sold locally; lack of transport precluded travel to other markets.

The women believed that the initiative was worthwhile: it gave them a chance to earn an income, and offered them, as refugees, some stability. A day-care centre, built with the help of OXFAM, UK, enabled them to work without worrying about their children. And, importantly, the pressing problem of providing food to families in an area of famine was beginning to be solved.

Source: Mutemba (ed.), 1985.

REFERENCES

Agarwal, Bina, *Cold Hearts and Barren Slopes: The Woodfuel Crisis in the Third World* (London: Zed Books; New Delhi: Allied Publishers, 1986).

Ahmed, Iftikhar, *Technology and Rural Women: Conceptual and Empirical Issues*, (London: Allen & Unwin, 1985).

Arizipe, Lourdes, and Josefina Aranda, "Women Workers in the Strawberry Agribusiness in Mexico", in Eleanor Leacock and Helen Safa (eds), *Women's Work: Development and the Division of Labor by Gender* (South Hadley, Massachusetts: Bergin & Garvey, Inc., 1986).

Bamba, Nonny, "Ivory Coast: Living with Diminishing Forests", in *Women and the Environmental Crisis*, Report of the Proceedings of the Workshops on Women, Environment and Development, Nairobi, 10–20

July 1985 (Nairobi: Environment Liaison Centre, 1985).

Bandyopadhyay, L., and Vandana Shiva, *Drought Development and Desertification,* Brief Report on the 2-day Seminar on the Control of Drought Desertification and Famine, held at India International Centre (New Delhi, 17–18 May 1986, 1986).

Barry, Jessica, "Oxen: a Women's Best Friend?", in *Earthscan Bulletin,* April (1986).

Brakel, Manus van, (1986). "Het is belangrijk uit te gaan van onze eigen kennis en technieken. Boeren en Boerinnen uit de Derde Wereld (2)", *Milieudef-ensie,* vol. 15, no. 1 (1986).

Braun, Arnelle, "The First Person You See is a Buffalo", in Ceres, Special issue on "Food, Agriculture and Women" (Rome: FAO, 1984).

Bull, David, *A Growing Problem: Pesticides and the Third World.* (Oxford: Oxfam, 1982).

Chaney, Elsa, *Subsistence Projects for Rural Women* (Kellogg Institute, 1985).

Creevey, Lucy (ed.), *Women Farmers in Africa: Rural Development in Mali and the Sahel.* (Syracuse, NY: Syracuse University Press, 1986).

Dankelman, Irene, "Vrouwen, Milieu en Ontwikkeling", *Nieuwsbrief Milieu and Ontwikkeling,* vol. 3 (4) (1985).

Davies, Miranda, *Third World – Second Sex: Women's Struggles and National Liberation* (London: Zed Press, 1983).

Eviota, Elizabeth U., "The Articulation of Gender and Class in the Philippines", in Eleanor Leacock and Helen Safa (eds), *Women's Work: Development and the Division of Labor by Gender* (South Hadley, MA: Bergin & Garvey, Inc., 1986).

FAO, *Agriculture: Toward 2000* (Rome: FAO, 1981).

FAO, "Women are Farmers too", News Release, February (1986) *Feminist Theory, State Policy and Rural Women in Latin America,* Kellogg Institute Working Paper, no. 49 (Notre Dame: December 1985).

Foster, Theodora, *A Common Future for Women and Men (and All Living Creatures): a submission to the World Commission on Environment and Development.* EDPRA Consulting Inc., Ottawa, Canada, 31 March (1986).

Fresco, Louise, "Vrouwen en Landbouwontwikkeling; de stand van zaken 10 jaar no Mexico", in *Geen Oplossingen zonder Vrouwen.* NCO Platformbijeenkomst Plattelandsontwikkeling en de Positie van de Vrouw, Arnhem, 24 April (1985).

Guazzelli, Maria José, "Southern Brazil: Breaking with an Imposed Dependence", in *Women and the Environmental Crisis.* Report of the Proceedings of the Workshops on Women, Environment and

Development, Nairobi, 10–20 July 1985 (Nairobi: Environment Liaison Centre, 1985).

Gubbels, P.A., and A Iddi, *Women Farmers: Cultivation and utilization of soybeans among West African women through family health animation efforts. Case Study* (Oklahoma City: World Neighbours, 1986).

Huston, Perdita, *Third World Women Speak Out.* (Davao City, Philippines: Asian Women's Research and Action Network, 1985).

ICDA, "Traditional Varieties: the Testimony of a Farmer", ICDA *News Special Report: Seeds,* July (1985).

IFDP, "Rural Women's Research Team, *Tough Row to Hoe: Women in Nicaragua's Agricultural Cooperatives* (San Francisco: IFDP, 1980).

ILO-INSTRAW, *Women in Economic Activity: a Global Statistical Survey (1950–2000).* (INSTRAW: Statistical Publication no. 10, 1985).

ISIS, *Women in Development: A Resource Guide for Organization and Action.* SISI Women's International Information and Communication Service (Geneva: ISIS, 1983).

Jiggins, Janice, "Food Production and the Sexual Division of Labour; Policy and Reality", unpublished paper, 1984).

Lappé, Frances Moore, and Joseph Collins, *Food First* (New York: Ballantine, 1978).

Lappé, Frances Moore, and Joseph Collins, *World Hunger: Twelve Myths* (New York: Grove Press; London: Earthscan, 1986).

Leon de Leal, Magdalena, "State Rural Development: Columbia", *Feminist Theory, State Policy and Rural Women in Latin America,* Kellogg Institute Working Paper, no. 49. University of Notre Dame, December (1985).

MAG, *Proyecto Determinación de Residueos de Pesticidas Clorados en Leche Materna.* Ministério de Agricultura y Canaderia y Consejo Nacional de Ciencia y Tecnologia. (Quito, December 1986).

Muntemba, S. (ed.), *Rural Development and Women – Lessons from the Field* (Geneva: ILO, 1985).

Nash, June, and Helen Safa *et al.*, *Women and Change in Latin America* (South Hadley, Bergin & Garvey Inc., 1986).

Netherlands IUCN Committee, *The Netherlands and the World Ecology: Towards a National Conservation Strategy in and by the Netherlands, 1986–1990* (Amsterdam: Netherlands National Committee for IUCN, 1986).

Non-Governmental Liaison Service, *Case Studies from Africa: Towards Food Security* (New York: United Nations, 1987).

Nyoni, Sithembiso, "Africa's Food Crisis: Price of ignoring Village Women?", in *Women and the Environmental Crisis*. Report of the Proceedings of the Workshops on Women, Environment and Development, Nairobi, 10–20 July 1985 (Nairobi: Environment Liaison Centre, 1985).

Pearce, Jenny, *Promised Land* (London: Latin American Bureau, 1986).

Poldermans, Caroline, "Rol van de Vrouw in Voedselproduktie wordt onvoldoende Onderkend", *Aspecten*, vol. 18 (6) 1986).

Sachs, Karin, "An Overview of Women and Power in Africa", in Jean F. O'Barr (ed.), *Perspectives on Power* (Durham, NC: Duke University Center for International Studies, 1982).

Shiva, Vandana, "India: the Abundance Myth of the Green Revolution", in *Women and the Environmental Crisis*. Report of the Proceedings of the Workshops on Women, Environment and Development, Nairobi, 10–20 July 1985 (Nairobi: Environment Liaison Centre, 1985a).

Shiva, Vandana, "Where has all the water gone? The case of water and feminism in India", in *Women and the Environmental Crisis*. Report of the Proceedings of the Workshops on Women, Environment and Development, Nairobi, 10–20 July (Nairobi: Environment Liaison Centre, 1985b).

Sinha, Rhadha, *Landlessness: A growing problem* (Rome: FAO, 1984).

Spears, J.S., *Wood as an Energy Source: the Situation in the Developing World*. Paper presented at the 103rd Annual Meeting of the American Forestry Association (Washington, DC: World Bank, 1978).

Taylor, Debbie *et al*, *Women: A World Report* (London: Methuen and New Internationalist, 1985).

UNEP, *Women, Environment and Food* (Nairobi: UNEP, 1980).

Weiss, Ruth, *Die Frauen von Zimbabwe* (München Frauenbuchverlag, Weissman Verlag, 1986).

Whitehead, Ann, "The Green Revolution and Women's Work in the Third World", in Wendy Fulkner and Erik Arnold (eds), *Smothered by Invention: Technology in Women's Lives* (London: Pluto Press, 1985).

Williams, Paula J., *The Women of Koundougou*. Hanover, USA: Institute of Current World Affairs, 1984).

World Council of Churches, "Women Ending Hunger", *Women in a Changing World* (Geneva: WCC, 1986).

World Resources Institute and International Institute for Environment and Development, *World Resources 1986* (New York: Basic Books, 1986).

31

2

WOMEN IN THE FIGHT AGAINST DESERTIFICATION
Marie Monimart

This chapter analyses the role of women in desertification control as described in forty-three studies carried out in six different countries of the Sahel: Burkina Faso, Cape Verde, Mali, Mauritania, Niger and Senegal.

Its purpose is to identify the factors contributing to *the economic, social and political advancement of women in the Sahel, from the standpoint of development and desertification control*. There are two basic postulates:

- the postulate put forward in the CILSS-club du Sahel strategy – that *rural development in the Sahel is inseparable from the fight against desertification;*
- the postulate that the mass migration of men from the countryside, exacerbated by the ecological disaster of desertification, makes the *specific advancement of women in the Sahel* a burning issue.

Against this background, women's participation in desertification control is a crucial issue for the subregion.

Our studies analyse the different approaches and projects involving women in working groups, and sometimes in the decision-making and leadership groups involved in anti-desertification programme and policies. We have deliberately chosen to analyse *positive desertification-control experiments* – positive from the technical standpoint and, as far as possible, positive from the social standpoint, although experiments of this kind are too recent to draw any definitive conclusions from them.

It was suggested beforehand that we approach the question in two ways: from the broader outlook of the whole village, and more specifically from the women's viewpoint. At the practical level, the fieldwork was carried out jointly with R.M. Rochette (PA CILSS), Ouagadougou), whose mission is to produce a publication on current successful desertification-control experiments in the Sahel, to be entitled "Le Sahel en Lutte contre la Désertification".

Three lessons may be drawn from these studies:

1. Sahelian women can and must put forward their viewpoint; but their ideas and opinions need to be listened to specifically, as men everywhere have recognized.
2. The fight against desertification in the Sahel can be won, but only if women's part in the fight is recognized as being of prime importance:
    • in quantitative terms, because the women remain permanently on the land abandoned by the migrating men;
    • in qualitative terms, through their stubborn insistence on staying on their home ground and holding back the disappearing earth, men and water.
3. Desertification has engendered or accelerated some destructive, disruptive trends, but it has also set up a dynamic which may lead to positive changes. Sahelian women have understood this.

It is for these reasons that it would be more than a mistake to exclude Sahelian women from rural development and anti-desertification schemes, ignore them or marginalize their participation; it would mean failure in any attempt to establish a new socioecological balance in the Sahel, in a durable manner and before it is too late.

WOMEN IN THE FACE OF DESERTIFICATION

Women experience desertification as a *radical, irreversible disruption*. They are lucid on the subject: over the past twenty years, and particularly since 1984, all hope of a return to the pre-1968 situation has vanished.

While most see desertification as "a curse, the source of our suffering", the women do not see the will of God or the hazards of the climate as the sole *cause*; they willingly accept the responsibility of individuals and rural communities in the process of ecological degradation.

The newest and most significant trend is their *growing awareness of the negative effects of population growth on living conditions and the environment*. The old women are the sharpest critics of the rising birth rate, especially in areas of high population density like the Mossi plateau.

Women perceive the desertification phenomenon in a comprehensive way, linking cause and effect as they analyse its ecological and socioeconomic impact. For all three main agroecological zones – Saharo-Sahelian, Sahelian and Sudano-Sahelian – the women list the consequences, in order of importance, as follows:

- they unanimously denounce the *increase in domestic labour* that goes hand in hand with *deforestation, an increased birth rate* and *scarcity of water*;
- they stress how they have *woken up to the situation and organized themselves*, positive consequences of their openness to questions involving the whole village community, e.g. CES.DRS initiatives and the creation of *new activities*;
- they complain of the *worsening migration of the menfolk* to the towns and the serious social upheavals this entails;
- they stress the *impoverishment* due to falling agricultural output and degradation of the land, which is felt more sharply than food or water shortages.

But one must beware of this apparent unanimity across the main agroecological zones, since a zone-by-zone analysis shows marked differences in women's perceptions of desertification, always with close reference to the ecological and human environments. In the Saharo-Sahelian zone, where the environment has deteriorated most, its socioeconomic effects – and first and foremost the exodus of the men – are far more predominant in the women's replies than they are in the other two zones, where the women's concern is more evenly divided between ecological and socioeconomic effects.

Degradation of the environment penalizes women especially, in all fields, but particularly in the domestic tasks that are so essential to group survival:

- *Fuelwood supplies* have become a real problem – indeed, a severe problem – in most regions of the Sahel. With deforestation and the extension of prohibitions, fuelwood has to be gathered further and further from the villages. Fuel-gathering, a job that has to be done several times a week, becomes ever more time-consuming and burdensome, to the point of becoming unbearable.
- While *water shortage* is no new phenomenon in the Sahel, it has reached critical proportions in many places. Asked what their biggest problems are, women in all three zones almost always list the deadly three: *water, wood, grinding of grain*. The women sometimes have to go at night to the well, where the wait is interminable. Water-carrying is a tremendous waste of time and energy.
- *The degradation and reduced availability of cultivable land* penalizes the women particularly. Two contradictory trends emerge: on the one hand the women are allocated increasingly marginal plots of land, or refused land altogether; while on the other hand the departure of the men leaves them with new responsibilities and tasks as more and more women find themselves acting alone as head of the family farmholding, in fact if not in law. *Desertification brings the land-ownership issue into sharp relief for women.*
- *The land and the women alike are exhausted.* Neither gets any rest; women's work on the farm has increased; falling yields and the adoption of cash crops force them to work harder and produce more cereals on their own plots, to the detriment of their usual crops.
- *The gathering of wild plant products* accounts for a high proportion of women's incomes and provides nutritional supplements

for the entire family. But desertification, deforestation and overuse of wilderness areas have drastically reduced the amount of supplementary products gathered in the bush. As the women so eloquently put it, *"The trees have turned mean"*, and all their natural produce, such as vegetable butter or "soumbala", is severely affected.

Wild or cultivated, then, the land no longer feeds herds or humans: scarcity, and in the worst years famine, settle in. The women, children and old people are the worst affected.

- The women's *craftwork activities* are threatened too: cotton hardly grows any more on the Mossi plateau, and the women are being forced to reduce or abandon their spinning; doum palm and andropogon leaves are disappearing from the village lands, forcing the women to go dozens of kilometres for their raw materials or give up a source of income that is increasingly necessary to buy food for the family. Even traditional house-building, a women's job in herding communities, is under threat.

Thus the cumulative ecological impact of desertification has severely affected women's daily lives in the Sahel. Access to the essential sources of life has become uncertain and even, in the case of wood supplies, prohibited and punishable. The dry season, once a time when the pace of work slowed down, is now devoted to intense activity merely for survival, giving women no chance to rest before the hard work of the cropping season begins again. As the women modestly say, "Life has become hard".

Socioeconomic effects

While they must suffer the ecological effects of desertification, Sahelian women are even more sensitive to the socioeconomic disruptions these effects provoke or accentuate, the foremost of these being the *departure of the men*.

- Besides the traditional work-related migration, an old and well-organized practice, there is now *drought migration*, a response to emergency situations, especially in the Saharo-Sahelian zone.

Their herds decimated, many herders have joined the flood of *"drought victims"* pouring into miserable camps on the outskirts of the towns or in the "asphalt villages" of Mauritania. While the men leave to try their luck in the towns, the women, old people and children stay on, abandoned, to wait for food aid. Asphalt and aid together encourage the men to leave, as the family's food needs seem to be assured in their absence.

- *Migration for work* is amplified by desertification, and the centres of immigration are further and further away, since the nearest coastal countries (Côte d'Ivoire, Nigeria) are becoming saturated: now men are travelling as far as Cameroon, Gabon, Zaire or Europe. They stay away for longer periods, no longer return for the cropping season every year, and sometimes emigrate for good. Some young women also take the migrant's road, alone or with their husbands.

For the women, the mass exodus of the men is the most painful result of desertification. It has turned hundreds of thousands of women into "widows", left without news of their menfolk for years on end. All they can do is wait, while their parents grow older and their children grow up fatherless, merely waiting to reach the age when they too can leave.

The mass exodus of the men has created *a chain of social destabilization effects*, especially in the Saharo-Sahelian zone. The destructuring – or, indeed, disintegration – of certain societies, nomadic pastoral societies especially, and the profound changes affecting all the traditional societies, leave populations in a state of bewilderment, incapable of finding a response to their new situation.

- The first result is a profound *destabilization of marriage patterns*: the normal ratio of men to women in the bush is disrupted. This has brought contradictory trends and led to later marriage in some cases, earlier marriage in others. In the Saharo-Sahelian zone one is beginning to find single women of twenty or older; some have lost all hope of marrying. The young men cannot pay the dowry and must leave home to acquire the money. Elsewhere, families are forced by poverty into marrying off fifteen-year-old girls to merchants for a derisory sum. Long periods of separation lead to *unstable marriages*. Polygamy is developing in societies where it was previously rare, whilst more and more women find themselves alone with dependent children after a fleeting relationship – abandoned, repudiated or divorced. Marriage no longer necessarily brings security.

- Some young people are beginning to reject the hard conditions of village life and to rebel against the labour and destitution that are their lot. These are the *"disobedient children"* – boys who do not want to dig the fields, girls who refuse to grind the grain or join the interminable queue at the well. The parents have no way of forcing them to obey, for the young people threaten to leave the village and abandon them. Demands for a new sexual freedom often lead to illegitimate pregnancies, resulting either in early marriage or in the girl's departure for the city.

The women must also face up to *growing individual and family poverty*. The loss of the herd, lower yields, increasing scarcity of wild plant products and the departure of the men have led to the ruin of some population groups and destroyed the traditional channels of trade and barter. In the bush, *destitution is a day-to-day reality*: famine forces people from their land, but they try to stay put and resist want and hunger by developing *survival strategies* and waiting for better days. They sell their family belongings, often at derisory prices; they no longer have any reserves of goods or livestock.

The women too must strip themselves of their belongings: livestock, jewellery, furniture. Moreover, they are obliged to spend more and more time in the family's fields, to the detriment of their own crops and their trading or craftwork activities. *Their health*, that precious asset, *is severely undermined* by privation of food, more frequent pregnancies, and the increasing burden of work.

The process of desertification has thus hastened the breakdown of socioeconomic structures in societies undergoing forced change. The socioeconomic role of the women is also weakened: their role as educators and counsellors is affected by the length of time they spend on everyday tasks that have now become a struggle for survival.

Despite this appalling list of negative effects from desertification, the vast majority of Sahelian women (91 per cent) have *stressed two positive effects* on their situation: *a new awareness and organization, and the creation of new activities.*

In most Sahelian societies, it is clear that the exercise of responsibility, the power of decision and access to the means of production, are in the hands of the men. But the desertification crisis has forced the men to leave, and the women now find they have decisions to take, new responsibilities to carry out and new tasks to accomplish.

- This *"awakening"* is first reflected in the *demand for information*. The fight against deterioration of the land has become everybody's business: *"the women have got to their feet and are trying to halt this destruction"*. The need for men and women to work together sometimes takes precedence over the old sexual division of labour. The demographic weight of women in the villages means that the men are obliged to take them into account, and the fact that they stay permanently in the villages makes it easier for them to obtain education and training.
- The women have understood that, to make themselves heard, they must *come together in modern organizations* – women's groups or co-operatives – larger, more powerful and more respected by government services or projects than their traditional forms of organization. These new groups, which sometimes embrace all the women in the village, have asserted themselves to the point of becoming fully fledged representational bodies in the decision-making structures of the village, whatever their actual nature and sociopolitical character may be. The woman who chairs the women's group is an authority. Organized and united, *the women's group is an official interlocutor* capable of putting forward its demands.

Organized and recognized, the women in a women's group wish to undertake *new activities*: collective or individual farming, market gardening, craftwork, small-scale trade, drought-control schemes, etc. The activities of the women's groups are still specific, one-off initiatives, often with very low profit levels, but they are seen as helping to improve the present situation and as representing a hope for the future.

The price the women pay for desertification is all the higher for the fact that they are always there, on the land, and have no means of escape. Their increasing consciousness of their situation is beginning to arouse positive, constructive reactions on their part: not only do they participate on a massive scale in anti-desertification schemes, they also want to be informed, to organize, to start new economic activities; it is they who are the most frank and open on the population issue. They speak of the fight against desertification in terms of survival, their own and their children's, and of bringing back to the village the disappearing earth, water and men.

WOMEN AND THE FIGHT AGAINST DESERTIFICATION

Throughout the Sahel, women are playing a major part in desert-ification control; but what precisely this part is must be clearly understood, and the basic question to ask is *whether present anti-desertification policies help advance the socioeconomic position of women through the projects undertaken, or whether they merely make use of their labour.*

Our descriptive analysis of women's participation in anti-desert-ification schemes shows that *they are physically involved to a huge extent*. More often than not they make up more than 50 per cent of the workforce on a project, and this proportion may reach 95 per cent in reforestation projects like the PDRI project in Keïta, Niger. Women's massive participation in the workforce on anti-desertification schemes is only partly due to the departure of the men; the women also have their own motivation.

Their participation is also very *varied*:

- reforestation and tree nursery work;
- CES.DRS site work;
- construction of improved cookstoves;
- out-of-season cropping;
- various activities, e.g., fattening livestock, manure pits, improved farming methods, etc.

They carry out a wide range of tasks: fetching water and meals for site workers, general labour (mainly fetching stones, earth or water). As a rule they are given *the least skilled, most arduous jobs*. Some, however, are beginning to get the benefit of specific training in the use of water levels for tracing contour lines, in tree nursery techniques, construction and maintenance of improved cookstoves, market gardening or arboriculture. Very few are given jobs with responsibility.

In most cases the women *volunteer* for the work, driven by their strong desire to restore the land, to have the right to land and water, and to hold back the exodus of the men. They feel they are working for their children's future, and they are aware that the fight against desertification is a long-term task. They express pride at taking part in a collective job, alongside men or in place of the absent men. On the other hand, there are too many cases where women participate *under indirect pressure* of one kind or another, e.g. to save the family's land or benefit from mass distribution of food aid. In many cases, women are still being excluded from anti-desertification schemes, or ignored.

The most widespread form of participation is *unpaid*; but the women may receive *food aid* of one kind or another; "food for work" in the form of daily food rations or meals onsite. *Waged work* is far less common; it is usually men who take all the waged jobs available. Two interesting cases were found in Cape Verde, where the workers were paid, and in Burkina Faso, where a few teams of women were on waged work building bunds.

All in all, women participate in anti-desertification schemes on a massive scale, forming a majority of the workforce, working voluntarily, unpaid, and on underskilled tasks. Various approaches are employed in such schemes, and the approach is the determining factor.

Our overall analysis of the *approaches* employed in the cases studied shows no significant difference between the different types of agency involved (bilateral or multilateral aid agency, NGO) or between the different types of project (large-scale or small) as far as integrating women into the project is concerned. On the other hand, the ten most successful experiments show that women are better integrated in projects with an all-round approach than they are in single-issue projects. The all-round projects generally include a women's scheme, either as an integral part of the main project or alongside it; the single-issue projects do so less often. On the other hand, few specific women's projects so far have included desertification control within their scope.

The role of the project management is decisive, and agencies and projects differ little in this respect. The most successful experiments show a high supervision ratio and frequent supervision, involving outside managers in close collaboration with the government services in all activities. *Management and supervision by women is the key to any approach to women's participation*, but this is far less concentrated than the male management levels, and is satisfactory in only 40 per cent of the cases studied, as against 90 per cent for the ten most successful experiments. With management by women, *women's self-management* emerges: the training of women "relay supervisors" permanently based in the area is one satisfactory response that holds great promise for the future.

Projects carried out with women too often suffer from a care-orientated approach (health, grain mills) and are not always carried out with a view to development, socioeconomic advancement and restoration of the environment. This general trend is remedied to a significant extent where there is a specific women's side to the project: in the ten most successful experiments, higher percentages are obtained for all work undertaken with women where there are women managers and suitable, specific schemes for the women.

Implementation of these schemes implies taking an interest

in the issue of *women's training and organization*. As a part of projects undertaken at village level, there are three possible approaches: women can be excluded from part or all of the work undertaken; they can be integrated into joint activities with the men; or one can work specifically with the women as a group.

- It is still common to exclude women from pilot activities in projects and schemes, and from any allocations of land, agricultural extension services, and access to credit or training.
- However, an unsegregated approach is becoming increasingly common, especially in Burkina Faso; this may be due to the numbers and scale of anti-desertification projects under way and the energy of the women's groups in that country. In fact, most anti-desertification projects could not be carried out successfully without the women. Women are beginning to receive training alongside men, but male resistance is strong, among villagers and project managers alike. Even so, male resistance can be fought, as is shown by the work of the local Burkinabe "Vive le Paysan" Association, which has made huge efforts to train women in a non-exclusive context.
- Specific training for women is still by far the most common form. It is justified in some cases by sociocultural constraints, or where the work to be done concerns only the women.

There is unfortunately no need to demonstrate that women are lagging behind in terms of training and education. The logic behind specific support for women's groups should lead to a combined approach, working jointly with men and women and working specifically with women. This combined approach seems to be the most fruitful, though it must be borne in mind that the first criterion of success in a project is its capacity to take account of the particularities of the human and ecological environment in which it is operating.

The Projects: An Assessment

We need to ask to what extent women's participation in the fight against desertification brings a response to their needs and helps towards their socioeconomic advancement.

In their work on anti-desertification sites, the disadvantages women suffer are greater than the advantages they gain.

Providing unskilled manual labour in 83 per cent of cases, unpaid in 65 per cent, women do none the less draw some benefits, both material and sociocultural, from their participation in site work:

- The *material benefits* depend on the form of participation: often food aid, either in the form of daily rations or as meals served onsite. Wages remain a rare but much-prized form of payment.
- The *socio-cultural benefits* are much appreciated. Because women's help was needed, their isolation has been broken; they have been kept informed about the projects to be undertaken, and this meets their demand for information. Participation in site work has instigated or strengthened women's organizations and the cohesion and sense of responsibility of women's groups. Mixed sites have led to changes in the traditional sexual division of labour. Some women have had the benefit of training in a specific technical task. Training schemes and intervillage encounters have been organized. Sometimes, too, it is women's groups that have been the main protagonists in a scheme to combat desertification. The impact of such schemes is considerable, for the village community as much as for the women.

These benefits do not make the women forget that they also suffer considerable disadvantages:

- In the first place they condemn the *excessive increase in their workload*. The day's work on the site is in addition to an exhausting day of domestic labour.
- Women also complain that *the work is extremely arduous*: for hours on end, they must carry heavy loads on their heads or handle stones and tools.

- The work can have serious *effects on the health of mothers and children*: pregnant or breastfeeding women spend the day at work on the site, their babies on their backs: childcare is rarely organized for the infants.
- *Massive food aid*, far from helping to stem the *migration of the men*, can even encourage it. A man will leave the village all the more easily if his family's food is "guaranteed" by the work of the women and children on a project site.
- Women's participation in site work may *hinder other activities* such as cotton-spinning or basket-weaving, resulting in a loss of income.
- Lastly, although there has been progress on the issue, women suffer *inequality of treatment in information and training*. Where a project site involves men and women, few trained women are able to apply their new know-how on the site. Their decision-making power remains very limited: on most anti-desertification sites, their labour-power alone is put to use.

The anti-desertification projects   Women benefit only to a limited extent from the desertification-control projects undertaken:

- Access to water is of immediate satisfaction to all, for example where a dam is built: gardens can be created and household water requirements are met.
- But newly available or newly productive land *raises a major problem of land-ownership and control* for women:
- 84 per cent of CES.DRS operations have made it possible to recover land, but women have acquired individual property rights over land in only 6 per cent of cases, although they were in a clear majority in the project workforces.
- Because the women do not own their fields, which are in any case small and poorly sited, these fields are affected little, or not at all, by CES.DRS projects.
- The owners of the fields allocated to the women often oppose any anti-erosion or planting work on them, for fear of losing their rights to the land: this is a major obstacle to women taking up agroforestry and CES.DRS techniques.

–   Where an area is irrigated, women do not usually receive plots.

In the long run, there is a great danger of demobilizing the women. Yet they seem to compensate by getting the community to allocate land to the women's group in the form of a common field, a garden or a plantation.

- As regards *agricultural production*, the most positive development is the spread of fruit-growing and market gardening among women's groups. But women's access to agricultural extension services and to the factors of production is still very limited and extremely unequal: the basic problem is that few schemes and projects regard women as fully fledged agricultural producers.
- As regards *reforestation*, women are enthusiastic partisans of agroforestry and individual plantations. But their access to the new trees and tree products is even more limited than the men's. Reforestation operations that have succeeded with women are those in which their right to the trees is unambiguously guaranteed.
- Extension work on *improved cookstoves* is the anti-desertification activity that has most affected women. They are very open to any saving of wood, and to greater comfort and safety in their cooking area. In regions that are badly deforested, and where the scheme has been well conducted, women's commitment to the stoves is total. But all too often the schemes are hasty affairs: no work to arouse awareness, no training, and above all no follow-up. Furthermore, schemes and projects sometimes use initiation into the new cookstoves merely as a way of integrating women into the fight against desertification; worst of all, such schemes can be used as an excuse to exclude the women from the production project. Women's participation in desertification control cannot and must not be limited to use of improved cookstoves.

Where anti-desertification schemes are concerned, there are still too many constraints and deficiencies for women to be unreservedly won over to the techniques applied. Moreover, one can see that women are too often the victims of contradictions or overlap between different schemes: participating as volunteers or under pressure, they have to take part in every project launched in the village by outside agencies. This can mean a ridiculously heavy additional workload, and can have a very demoralizing effect. *Forgotten by one project, submerged by another, women need a minimum of coherence in approaches to desertification control.* This disappearing assessment, however, should be viewed with a sense of proportion: this type of project is a very recent development.

Women urgently need to develop their minor activities of *trade, craftwork*, etc., and these call for appropriate *loan facilities*. It is clear that by bringing a response to these demands, the anti-desertification projects would encourage and broaden women's participation in environmental restoration activities. Pressure on the environment can be reduced, on the one hand, by improving production techniques, product quality and marketing. Lastly, by encouraging women to produce raw materials (planting, protecting naturally regenerated growth, exploiting resources rationally) one will help both the environment and the women. The situation in the Sahel is such that without the help of appropriate loan facilities it is difficult for women to develop their trading or craft activities. Yet it is well known, and confirmed by experience, that women are reliable borrowers.

Experience also shows that schemes to lighten domestic labour (village water supplies, mills, etc.) and to improve living conditions in the villages (health facilities, a village shop) free women's labour-power and improve their living conditions. But this does not seem to have been understood, for activities of this kind are recorded in only 42 per cent of cases, whereas women are given a heavy additional workload on the anti-desertification sites and the hardness of life in the village encourages the young to leave.

Our assessment is, overall, negative. It has to be conceded that at the present time, desertification-control policies regard women as secondary and provide no advancement for them. Although they participate on a massive scale and in many different ways, most schemes and projects do no more than use their labour-power, relegating them to the most arduous and least skilled jobs.

However, some promising trends are developing: the massive scale of women's participation is a positive factor; and women's organizations have acquired renewed energy and strength to meet the needs of the fight against desertification. Training schemes are beginning to cover men and women together, and an anti-desertification project can be a powerful unifying factor in the village, improving the division of tasks and responsibilities.

For many women, combating desertification is the way forward to improve their living conditions, keep the men at home and prepare for their children's future. *But one cannot continue to exploit their labour while denying this hope.* This has been understood by some projects which are running innovative experiments to integrate women into the fight against desertification.

THE LESSONS OF THE MOST POSITIVE EXPERIMENTS

To be able to assess a successful environmental restoration or reforestation scheme, it is important to know and understand, first of all, *the relationship between women and local plant life*, and how this has changed.

Whichever agroecological zone we look at, gathering wild produce is a fundamental part of women's socioeconomic role. Women transmit from mother to daughter the knowledge and know-how that once helped to preserve a certain equilibrium with the surrounding vegetation. But this equilibrium has been broken by a number of interacting factors than constitute a veritable *spiral of destruction*. Population growth has accentuated pressure on the environment and led to an increase in gathering activities, at the same time as the bush is reduced by the expansion of the cultivated areas. The drop in agricultural productivity has led to scarcity and impoverishment, and the bush has been taxed even more heavily to provide a now indispensable food supplement and source of income (sale of fruit, raw materials for craftwork). The trees are overexploited and mutilated; tree populations have aged. Under pressure of necessity and emergency, the women have had to give up the traditional practices that helped to preserve the environment; they can no longer choose between species, and their knowledge is being lost. It is facile to say, as one high-level expatriate project manager did: "It's the women who cause desertification: they cut the wood, and they have the children."

Women prefer *local, multipurpose species*. Trees are used for two main purposes, *food and medicine*, before they are used for fuel. Women's predilection for wild fruit trees attests to the nourishment these trees provide. Traditional medicine holds a very important place in villages remote from modern chemists' shops, whose medicines are in any case often beyond the reach of country people. These needs have not always been understood by forestry workers, who still tend to favour species grown for timber and fuel. Women's demands are complementary, not contradictory: needs are no longer covered in certain areas, and anxiety is growing.

It is also important to stress the *educational role of women* in transmitting knowledge of trees and plants. It is the mother who initiates her children in the ways of the environment, in the great classroom of the bush – often the only classroom the children know. Folk tales teach, for example, that one must respect the trees if one hopes to benefit from their generosity; it is important that this kind of knowledge be recognized and continue to be transmitted. It is also vital for the women, who will pass on good or bad ways of treating the environment, to be informed and educated.

Positive experiments in reforestation that have really involved women as partners, and taken account of their demands and the constraints upon them, are still rare.

The experience of the *Azel craft co-operative* in Air, Northern Niger, is representative of the Saharo-Sahelian zone. Impoverished by drought, the women increased their production of plaited mats made of doum palm leaves. The result was overexploitation of the doum palms and a drop in the price of the mats. At the same time, the demand for the raw material grew and the price of the leaves rose. Destruction of the trees accelerated and spread. In 1984, with the aid of the Catholic Mission and the small religious community at Azel, the women formed a co-operative to produce a different type of craft product geared towards the urban and tourist markets. Using far less of the raw material, they made more elaborate goods that brought in significantly higher profits. At the present time the scheme is trying to involve the women in regenerating the doum palm groves. A consciousness-raising drive has been launched, with the help of the Telloua valley riverside biology protection project, and a 50 per cent revival is spoken of. The aim of the forestry agents (to plant doum palms) and the aim of the women (to have the leaves they need for their products) are convergent, not contradictory. But two battles remain to be won: to convince the forestry experts that this form of craft production is less destructive than the old one, and to convince the women that they must take part in the planting of the palms if they are to continue their craft activities. This experience is relevant for the entire Saharo-Sahelian zone.

At *Boulhazar*, in the Assaba region of Mauritania, some 300 women, who have recently become sedentary, have set up a flourishing craft co-operative. They have decided to launch into *market gardening and date palm production*. They have bought and equipped a plot of land for the purpose, for a total investment of FCFA 1 million. They have boldly bought forty date palm seedlings at FCFA 5,000 each, along with henna plants, etc. All these trees will provide a source of income in the long run. With some commercial wisdom the women have seen that permanent settlement in the region is inevitable, and they are preparing for the future in those terms. The way these women, once confined to their nomads' tents, have taken in hand the long-term development of the land where they have settled is a lesson in hope and energy. They believe their men will come home and that, thanks to this kind of effort, they will want to come back and live in their home village. The success of schemes like this is very important for the interior of the country, which is losing its population.

Women's tree nurseries are being launched. The women of the Fazenda Tarrafal co-operative in the north of Santiago Island, Cape Verde, decided to set up their own nursery. After training by the forestry department, they produced 10,000 seedlings which were bought by the forestry department, highly satisfied with a quality product involving less in the way of transport costs. The experiment is to be repeated next year, to the mutual satisfaction of the parties involved.

At Tessaoua in Niger the NGO Care International, involved in an agroforestry project in the area, has launched an experiment in individual private mini-nurseries with the women. The scheme is designed to meet two needs: the project wanted seedlings produced by private enterprise, and the women wanted trees and a source of income. The principle of the initiative is simple: *free enterprise and voluntary participation*. Each women chooses the number and species of seedling she wishes to raise at home, and she uses them however she likes: selling at her own price, giving them away, keeping them for her own use. Though modest in scale, this experiment can be regarded as a success, and it shows that town women can be interested in trees as well. Its success is due to three factors: the freedom of choice left to the women, the very close self-management that ensured constant monitoring of the scheme, and the decision to keep to a small scale. In the long run, only a few women will become expert and make their mini-nurseries a lasting activity.

More and more, women are showing their desire to grow the trees that will be useful to them. A women's tree nursery, or a nursery that takes account of women's demands, can be a starting point for agroforestry projects with women. Some projects are beginning to open their nurseries to women, and these initiatives are to be encouraged.

One experiment *involving women in the exploitation of forestry plantations* has been conducted in Cape Verde. Some large-scale plantations have reached the exploitation stage. The forestry department recruited and trained teams of workers to prune the trees; the wages were paid out of revenue from the prunings, sold by the kilo. The women proved to be the most efficient at pruning, and all-women teams formed. This is an interesting experiment in that it shows that women can manage wood resources rationally and can be reliable partners in a forestry project. Some projects, like the PARCE in Senegal and the PSUF in Guesselbodi, Niger, have begun to involve women. But all in all, these experiments are still too limited and too timid.

Rural agroforestry schemes, individual or collective, are beginning to be undertaken with the participation of women right across the Sahel. The *Gandiol area experiment* is the most innovative as regards woodlots for the women of the village. After the failure of a conventional village woodlot in 1984, the Gandiol area's autonomous dune-fixing project redefined the guidelines for its forestry scheme. The village woodlot became a hedged "demonstration woodlot" of 0.2 to 1 hectare, a multipurpose woodlot planted with a range of species and *created, maintained and managed by the women's groups* with the help of the rest of the population. A medicinal agroforestry scheme was run concomitantly, involving the traditional practitioners and the general population, and the protected species will gradually be reintroduced into the women's woodlots. It is also intended to create "health gardens" near the health-care centres, to supply medicinal plants for the traditional pharmacopoeia. The women are also involved in protection and natural regeneration of trees, *Acacia albida* especially.

This has proved a highly positive experiment: *the approach is centred on the women's groups, but in the name of the entire community and with its support*. The experiment is of far more than local significance, and all those agroforestry projects too exclusively focused on the male population could profit from it. It shows the part women can play in rural agroforestry in the Sahel, especially in areas where male emigration is high.

Services and projects have also begun, here and there, to *encourage individual plantations*. In Burkina Faso, the "Village Woodlot" project in Kaya has launched an initiative to help the spread of improved cookstoves: the women are being promised five tree seedlings per stove built. The operation has been a great success: 16,000 trees have been planted by individual women, and the project has not been able to fulfil all its promises. The same project, with backup from the forestry department, has trained "*women farmer/foresters*" whose role is to monitor the use of the improved cookstoves and to maintain the trees in their village. This initiative, costing little in relation to the cost price per hectare of the village woodlot, also provides a basis for women's self-management.

The results of all these experiments show that women are very much in favour of rural agroforestry schemes. But their support is hampered by two obstacles: the land tenancy problem and the right to the trees planted. If these obstacles were removed, the future of rural forestry in the Sahel would be largely in the hands of the women.

Lastly, *school* is a place where boys and girls can acquire a better knowledge of their environment and learn better behaviour towards it. In Mali, the school at Banakoroni near Ségou is raising young people's awareness through gardening activities, a tree nursery, embellishment of the living space, and an introduction to the improved cookstoves. The old men and women of the village have come along to lead these sessions. In Mopti, the International Union for the Conservation of Nature has created an environmental education and consciousness-raising course for schools. It publishes a quarterly bulletin about "Walia the Stork, messenger from our Nature", which is distributed in all the schools of the 5th Region. Experiments of this kind are not expensive considering their impact; and one must remember what a tragic shortage of teaching materials there is in Sahelian schools. Schools have something to learn from men and women of the bush.

The part women play in agricultural production has grown unceasingly over the past twenty years; this is due partly to the spread of cash crops, partly to the mass migration of the men, and partly to the modernization of agriculture, which has led to an increase in the area under cultivation.

The result has been a *change in the agricultural tasks and responsibilities that fall to women*. They work more in the family fields, sometimes to the detriment of their own fields, where they have for many years practised a diversified, intensive form of cropping. More and more often, as land for cultivation grows scarcer, the women are left without individual plots or forced to grow cereals on them. Lastly, male migration has made women responsible for the family farms in fact but not in law. Although they must carry out the work while the man is away, they do not receive the benefit of agricultural extension work or access to the factors of production.

The land-ownership and tenancy problem seems to be a major stumbling block. Women's access to land is inadequate in two respects, quantitative and qualitative. The length of time for which a plot is allocated is also uncertain. The allocation of land depends entirely on the men: husbands, owners, authorities. Moreover, custom has it that improving a plot or planting trees on it confers right of ownership. Owners generally oppose improvements, but they may also give permission for planting or other work and then take back the improved field. Under these conditions, it is hard to encourage women to undertake CES.DRS or agroforestry work in their fields. The great majority of schemes and projects back up the right of men to the land when improvements contribute to the spoliation of women.

However, women want individual appropriation of land. Because of the various ways their societies have been destabilized by desertification and the exodus of the men, they want to secure their access to the factors of production. Individual access remains very difficult, but collective appropriation is accepted better by the community. Desertification, and CES.DRS activities in the fields, reveal the problem of land-ownership to the women, and anti-desertification schemes involve a certain ambivalence: while individuals are excluded, land may be allocated to a collective groups.

Positive Experiments in Agriculture

Despite these handicaps, women are very much involved in CES.DRS activities. They are aware of the degradation of the land and its many consequences; they have invested their labour on a massive scale to save their threatened lands. The technique women have adopted most enthusiastically is that of *anti-erosion bunds* or banks, built of earth or stone. The experiment of Noogo in Yatenga is a good example of the teaching of this technique on the Mossi plateau. In two years, 115 hectares have been treated in this way, with the support of local and regional government services. Women have played a major part, making up 75 per cent of the labour force on the site. Site work is directed by a female development agent, and the organization of work is remarkable. The work has been divided among the different age groups: the oldest women mind the children in the shade, close to their mothers, who can stop to breastfeed in peace; the youngest women carry the stones, and the women of the middle age group arrange them along the contour lines or prepare the meal for the workers; everyone is entitled to a meal served onsite.

Noogo demonstrates three basic facts: that women have understood the need to combat desertification; that they know what they want and will adopt a scheme that responds to their needs; and that an anti-desertification site can retain a human dimension and need not resemble a forced-labour camp. *Consciousness-raising on the problems of environmental conservation has led to many other kinds of consciousness on the part of the women*: they want to restrict the number of children they have; they no longer cook without an improved stove; they have a collective field where they apply new farming techniques; in 1988 a manure pit scheme for men and women started up; they got together enough money to obtain a grain mill; for the first time, they have sent three little girls to the school in the next village; when at long last they have a well they mean to start a market garden; and they want to start a village shop with the profits from the mill.

The example of Noogo shows that a well-run anti-desertification scheme can open the way to rural development and the socioeconomic advancement of women, even if women are not the main beneficiaries from the measure taken. Yatenga provides many other positive examples. At Bassi, the women have been trained to build stone bunds and have formed *autonomous women's teams to build bunds for wages in other people's fields*. Teams of this kind have been launched in other villages: desertification control is beginning to create jobs in Yatenga!

Improvement of existing farming systems is also a part of the fight against desertification. In experiments where women have access to *agricultural extension work*, especially through work in their collective fields, their enthusiasm is obvious. Women are gradually being taught the use of manure or compost pits; *market gardening and arboriculture* are fast growing activities in most countries. The new vegetables are becoming a habitual part of the diet, and women consistently ask to take up market gardening, even in the Saharo-Sahelian zone.

Lastly, credit facilities to buy farm equipment, launch a trade venture, set up a mill, fatten sheep or acquire a cart or bicycle are being successfully launched by a variety of schemes and projects. The "Vive le Paysan" Association in Sapone has given loans to women's groups for animal-powered cultivation and storage of the shea-nut harvest to enable the women to withstand pressure from the traders.

The NGO ADRK is giving women access to its credit and savings co-operatives. At a later stage in the process the multiplication of women's groups also raises the problem of managing their money and farm produce: building small stores, or mini-grain banks, allows flexible, independent management of the women's harvests.

The problem of training lies at the heart of women's position as regards progress in farming. The "Vive le Paysan" Association has made great efforts in this direction; the "women farmer/foresters" of the village woodlot project at Kaya, and the ODIK project in Mali which intends to establish women "relay supervisors" at village level, are moving in the same direction. The project to support women's initiatives, under the aegis of the CMDT in the Koutiala region of Mali means to concentrate on schemes concerning management of women's agricultural activities, and to create a network of "women farmer/seed-multipliers". Lastly, support for *women's organizations* is beginning to develop.

The positive integration experiments are still too recent for definitive conclusions to be drawn; sometimes they show contradictory trends between different villages, or even within the same village. But the important thing is that a process is under way, and lessons can already be drawn from established failures and promising experiments. Although there are still too few, some anti-desertification experiments involving the socioeconomic advancement of women do exist, and they show the way forward. The battle is not yet won, but it is important to support such schemes where they exist, and to encourage others.

REPRODUCTIVE TASKS

Reproductive tasks include all the domestic tasks women carry out to ensure the reproduction of the family's labour-power, and pro-creation, the "production of producers". In terms of desertification control, the questions raised are how to save domestic energy and how to control population growth.

The Ninety-Hour Week

A hundred per cent of women's groups questioned mentioned an increase in domestic labour as a direct result of desertification. The three essential tasks that ensure the survival of the family – fetching water, fetching wood and preparing food – now take up most of the labour-power of Sahelian women in the dry season. A country woman's working day is fourteen hours long at the very least. As long as women have to use up the better part of their time and strength in the daily domestic grind, the way forward to development will remain closed to them.

In Sahelian conditions, women have long known how to avoid wasting water. Water is strictly managed, and small girls are taught the art from a very early age. The problems mentioned are the lack of means to raise water and transport it. Women need to be more closely involved in the well-management committee, and they need to be taught the simple maintenance jobs. Schemes and projects have made great efforts to provide village water supplies; these efforts must be continued until the water needs of all are met.

Women are unanimous in finding the daily or twice-daily job of *grain-grinding* a back-breaking task. The existence of grain mills, the increase in other household tasks (wood and water carrying) and increasing family size mean that women currently find it harder and harder to accept this task. Furthermore, they know that a well-run mill can make a profit. Senegal, among other countries, provides convincing evidence of this. A mill must not be presented as a gift, but as a money loan granted to the women for a profitable investment that will save them time and energy, and is certainly easier to install than a well. A grain mill is now an essential component of any improvement to village life.

The *scarcity of wood* and increasing prohibitions on the use of forestry resources have made the problem of wood supplies virtually insoluble in some regions. Fetching wood is becoming an unbearably arduous task. Women are reduced to burning crop residues and animal dung, thereby contravening regulations and risking heavy fines, or buying wood out of their meagre budgets. There are two ways of resolving the crisis: reducing wood consumption by using improved cookstoves or other energy sources; and changing the accessibility of wood supplies by appropriate regulations and the use of carts or bicycles for transport.

Traditional *house-building* in the Sahel is closely dependent on the availability of natural resources from the environment. The scarcity of raw materials and the increasing prohibitions on cutting timber leave country-dwellers no alternative: what other building method can they find at a time when family size is growing? Solutions may be found in rural agroforestry, involving appropriate species and a new attitude on the part of the forestry authorities, with greater responsiveness to the population's needs.

The excessive increase in their workload threatens the women's *educational role*. But this role is still essential since, despite governments' efforts, school attendance rates remain low, especially for girls. Overloaded with work, burdened with babies and toddlers, the mother finds it hard to fulfil her educational role. The girls are sacrificed; they do a servant's job, their work is indispensable to the household, and schooling becomes even more inaccessible to them. The overburdened women cannot always find the time to attend their own literacy sessions or training sessions – whose timetables are in any case not worked out to fit in with the women's. In this way, the increased workload threatens the future too: *the young women of the year 2000 are likely to be as illiterate as their mothers, without having had the chance to acquire their mothers' traditional knowledge*. To respond to the problem of education one must also respond to the problem of giving women more responsibility: the "ignorant" are excluded from decision-making structures. The circle must be broken. Cape Verde and Burkina Faso are developing some interesting experiments in rural childcare facilities. The fight against desertification cannot be restricted to reforestation schemes and anti-erosion work. It must also involve meeting demands for improved living conditions in the villages;

otherwise, the villagers will leave. And finally, it must mean putting an end to the unacceptable waste of women's energy.

Responses to the Energy Crisis

There is a fuelwood crisis in all parts of the region. Current reforestation efforts and attempts to save fuelwood are in danger of being completely annulled by population growth. In 1979, a *regional project for improved cookstoves* was launched by the Ecology/Environment Unit of the CILSS in Ouagadougou. Seven million Sahelian households are concerned by the problem of energy saving. Two new types of stove or cooking fire are currently being encouraged, both more efficient and better received by housewives than the old type: the improved, home-built, three-stone cooking fire and the portable metal or ceramic stove. Among the most advanced countries on this issue are Burkina Faso, Niger and The Gambia; at an intermediate stage are Senegal and Mali, while the least progress has been made in Mauritania and Chad. Cape Verde is a special case, since other energy sources are already in widespread use there. The project is reaching the end of its first phase, and is to broaden the scope of its activities to cover domestic energy sources.

The massive distribution of improved cookstoves in the country-side is a step forward, but certain reservations must be stated. Schemes to disseminate their use are too often evaluated in quantitative terms, whereas successful adoption of the stoves must be measured by other criteria: regular, correct use, maintenance and reconstruction. There are two key factors in successful use: training/awareness and, first and foremost, close monitoring of the schemes being run. Effective energy saving is hard to assess accurately. A survey of metal stoves, carried out in Niamey, shows considerable variations: 29 per cent savings where a stove is correctly used, compared to 3 per cent where it is not used rationally. Results from the three-stone stove can be even poorer. But the improved cookstoves should not be rejected for all that: in the first place, what has been saved has been saved; secondly, use of the new stoves forms new attitudes to fuel-saving. Properly run, backed up by donations of trees and provided with continual follow-up, a scheme to disseminate the use of these stoves wins total approval from the women.

While improved cookstoves on their own are not a solution to the fuelwood problem in the Sahel, they can help to slow down the crisis and, for the moment, they are the only alternative open to women in the countryside, who have no access to other energy sources. While gas is increasingly widely used in the towns, bottles and equipment are still expensive. Paraffin is used for lighting purposes only. Biogas and solar energy are as yet little used, though the women, tired of fetching firewood under present conditions, are far more open to the idea of new energy sources than is often thought. This impetus for change must be taken into account.

Gaining Control Over Population Growth

For more than thirty years the countries of the Sahel have been experiencing an unprecedented population explosion. Agricultural output has not kept pace with it, and *per capita* incomes have fallen. Long periods of drought and desertification have worsened the situation. Efforts to establish social infrastructures and conserve the environment may prove worthless if population pressure keeps up. As of now, fertility control is a pressing issue for most Sahel states.

State attitudes to population policies changed significantly during the decade from 1974 to 1984. 1984 was the year of the Arusha conference, with changes in governments' positions and the launching of family-planning projects combined with mother-and-child protection schemes. With the exception of Mauritania, most of the Sahel states recognize the need to control population growth, either to reduce the birthrate (in Cape Verde, Niger and Senegal) or to space births more widely and introduce mother-and-child protection (in Burkina Faso and Mali). Legislation has been introduced, allowing and encouraging the distribution of contraceptives. But implementation of government policy is hampered by negative attitudes that generally stem from the male population and from religion, and also by a ponderous administration and the lack of health or social infrastructures, though women are demanding birth control ever more loudly. New family health projects continue to spread, but they are far short of meeting women's needs, especially in the countryside, as the towns take priority in this matter.

Contrary to what is too often thought, country women overwhelmingly stress that increasing birth rate is an unwelcome problem. Births have become more frequent as *traditional practices have been neglected* (prolonged abstinence after a birth) and mother-and-child protection schemes have cut down infant mortality. The great majority of women would like to space their babies more widely, or indeed bear fewer children for the benefit of everyone, mothers, children and grandmothers. The older women are often the most open to change and the most determined to confront the men on a subject that is still taboo within the couple: "I am a grandmother and I want grandsons: but these puny little things wear a grandmother out; children must be allowed to grow" (from the Mossi plateau).

There is *a new feeling towards children* emerging nearly everywhere: the size of a family is no longer necessarily its strength, and a child no longer gives the parents a sure guarantee in the countryside: the departure or rebellion of the young has demonstrated this. Furthermore, *women want fewer children, better fed, properly cared for, properly dressed and educated.* It is therefore important to them to have the means to space out their babies, and their prime demand is for *information.* But the women also consider it essential to *involve the men in any attempt to raise awareness*, as it is the men who are most reticent and who have the power to decide. Access to contraceptives must be facilitated by all means, in terms of legislation and distribution alike. Family planning must be systematically combined with mother-and-child protection, for a child that is malnourished and sickly because its mother has borne too many babies in too short a time is the most powerful encouragement for a couple to adopt contraception; what is more, only if infant mortality drops significantly will parents be encouraged to limit the number of births. Lastly, the training of health workers, including rural midwives, is imperative if family planning is to be effectively disseminated.

The idea of control over population is now accepted by most of the Sahel states, but implementation of population policies is a slow and delicate process, and no slowdown in population growth can be expected in the short term. Country women are just as aware as women in the towns of the negative effects of population growth on their living environment; they need access to the means to limit their fertility at a time when they do most of the farm work and desertification-control work.

WOMEN AND GOVERNMENT POLICIES

Over the past twenty years women's condition has worsened considerably in Sub-Saharan Africa. Sahelian governments were not indifferent to the Women's Decade of 1975–85, and many adopted positions in support of women. At the top of the political tree there is talk of equality, emancipation, women's liberation, the need to integrate women into the development process. But one gets an unavoidable feeling that the heads of state are isolated on the issue: as the years go by, the language barely changes, doubtless because women's situation has not significantly changed either. Worn-out words suggest a certain statism: it has all been said, but little has been done. Creeping resistance combines with the obstacles that stem from a one-way respect for cultural, religious and national authenticity. Men are afraid of a real change in women – in *their* women. The country-wide situation is too often viewed in terms of urban women, who know and sometimes abuse their prerogatives, to the detriment of country women who are taking on an increasing share of the workload and responsibilities.

It is urgent, therefore, for the political will expressed in speeches to be translated into concrete measures, even though these will inevitably "upset current prejudices and attitudes", as Niger's most recent five-year plan puts it. But such legal or institutional measures will inevitably be unpopular with the male population on whom the government depends, and they therefore entail a degree of political risk. It has to be said that optimism is not widespread, even though some progress is being made.

The gap between discourse and action is no doubt most obvious in the *national women's associations*. There is often just one such organization, closely dependent on the political force in power – the UFB in Burkina Faso, the OMCV in Cape Verde, the UNFM in Mali, the SEM in Mauritania, the AFN in Niger, (Senegal is an exception). These women's organizations are often too dependent on the political powers to be able to serve women's interests fully. Mistrusted but enlisted to support the government, their hands are tied and they are pushed into the background. They are asked to give their approval – and, implicitly, the approval of all the country's women – to policy decisions in which they have played very little part. Short of resources, manpower and skills, they are easy to manipulate; their representation on decision-making bodies is more symbolic than real, and the men prefer to smile at the quaint traditions their contributions reflect rather than give them any real power to intervene or decide. Their structure is such that they can reach most of the women in the country, and they could be a powerful lever for the advancement of women if certain obstacles, fears and contradictions were eliminated among the male decision-makers. But the great majority of men, top-level executives included, have not yet decided in favour of genuine advancement for women and an unreserved involvement of women in the development process. The women themselves have not always become aware of how important a role they have to play nationally. Some of those at the top of the existing women's structures tend to pay more attention to their own privileges than to their "sisters in the countryside" or to women in more disadvantaged social strata. Intellectuals generally keep away from these associations, yet it is the task of the country's female elite to demonstrate the responsibility and competence the men are challenging them to prove. It would certainly be preferable for these monolithic organizations to open up to other structures, broaden the debate and strengthen women's representation in professional groups, cultural organizations, etc. Senegal's experience in this is exemplary.

The hesitancy of male decision-makers is reflected in the way implementation of a real plan of action on the issue is delayed. All too often, schemes are introduced in piecemeal fashion, with no coherent, concerted programme. It is vain to speak of promoting women's advancement unless a certain number of concrete measures are taken. The lifting of some major obstacles depends on the political level. Women's legal status must be clearly spelled out through family law, land law, and labour law, through subscribing to international agreements on the elimination of all discrimination against women, and so on. The coexistence of three systems of law – civil, religious and traditional – almost always operates against women, the men taking advantage of the women's ignorance. Clear choices need to be made regarding population policy, and women must be informed of their right to control their own fertility. The Sahel must not ignore the problem of the male veto over a wife's access to contraception. Measures to lighten women's tasks are indispensable, and must be governed by a nationwide policy.

Lastly, access to education and training is notoriously unequal. What skills will the Sahel's women be able to count on between now and the year 2000? If the situation is to move forward, it is vital to break the circle of ignorance and dependence.

The fight against desertification has become a priority in most of the Sahel states. The growing role of women in this fight is recognized; now it is urgent for states to define a policy of socioeconomic advancement for women, through their participation in desertification control. Because they remain permanently on the land while the men move out *en masse*, they hold a key position in agroforestry, land recovery and food security. Kept properly informed, they are the state's most reliable allies in the fight for control over population growth. Desertification can be halted only with their support.

CONCLUSION

Two major observations seem to be of crucial importance:

1. *The fight against desertification cannot be won unless women are recognized as the prime protagonists and their social and economic advancement is assured.* The current tendency – of using only their labour-power – runs a high risk of discouraging and demobilizing them in the long term, and this will lead to failure. Decision-makers and donors must reorientate their policies and anti-desertification projects to foster the advancement of women.
2. *The fight to gain control of population growth will be won in co-operation with the women,* who are the most lucid and open to the question of limiting family size for the well-being of all and the protection of the environment.

II

WOMEN AND THE FORESTS

3

RESTORING THE BALANCE: WOMEN AND FOREST RESOURCES
Food and Agriculture Organization of the United Nations

In non-industrial regions, trees are inextricably woven into the rural and household economies. They are used to provide fuel, fodder and food. They supply medicines and shade, increased soil fertility, shelter from the wind and protection from the rain. From them women fashion many of the products used in the house – and, often enough, the house itself. Perhaps most importantly of all, trees and forests provide many rural women with their only source of personal income.

TREES FOR FOOD

The home gardens of South-East Asia provide the most vivid illustration of the importance of trees in providing family food. Within perhaps 50 metres of each dwelling can be found bananas, coconuts, sugar apples, mangos, star apples, guavas, avocados, and breadfruit. In Indonesia, no fewer than thirty-seven species of fruit trees have been found growing in just one home garden. Even in societies in the Middle East, many women plant fruit trees within their walls.

Fruit is part of the regular diet of most people. But trees provide many other forms of nutrition. Nuts – high in both calories and protein – are an obvious example. Cashew nuts, in particular, are highly prized in many African countries. And in the Kalahari, the staple food of the Bushmen comes from the mongongo tree (*Ricinodendron digitata*), which provides both a fruit and a nut. The nut is roasted and, if necessary, stored.

The leaves, seeds, pods, sap and bark of trees form part of the diet of many rural people. The leaves of the baobab, rich in vitamins, are a major ingredient of the sauces served with starchy foods in some African countries. The vitamin-rich fruit from the same tree is known as monkey bread. The seeds from locust trees (*Parkia* species) are cooked like beans, or fermented and added to sauces. This food, which is rich in protein and fats, is known as dawa dawa in one African country and is much used in soup. The sap of palm trees is made into wine, while the seeds of other palms can be used as an oil that is important in providing energy and Vitamin A, lack of which causes eye lesions in small children. In the South-West Pacific, the pith of the sago palm is processed into a basic food, high in starch, that is used in the preparation of soups, cakes and puddings.

Trees also provide food in a number of indirect ways. For instance, rural people use nearby forests as an important source of both honey and edible fungi, a study in north-east Zambia found that what was catalogued as useless forest land was actually a major source of leafy wild vegetables and mushrooms, as well as caterpillars. These three items were major sources of protein and cash income; all three fall within women's responsibilities, and were processed or sold by women.

In nearly every society trees are used, either in the fields, in the homestead or both, as a means of increasing soil fertility, preventing soil erosion and altering micro-climates so that annual crops may grow better. In the fierce heat of some tropical countries, the shade that trees provide is essential to the survival of domestic animals.

Trees, directly and indirectly, thus provide rural women with a substantial portion of their families' diets. But they do more: they are often the only reliable source of food for the family when crops fail or during the lean periods between harvests. In Tanzania, two or three tree species are enough to provide some food for every month of the year. Research has shown that these trees are used more intensively during famines or droughts, illustrating their important role in providing food security. Furthermore, once established, trees need little care, and the food they provide often requires no effort other than picking or collecting. Much of the food that trees produce can also be stored without further processing.

Trees can provide produce at times of the year when annual crops never can, simply because their deep roots give them access to moisture throughout the year. The mango, for example, provides its fruit at the beginning of the rainy reason, when other crops are just being planted and the harvest is still distant. In the Sahel, pressure of work during planting can be so intense that there is not enough time to cook, and many families rely for nourishment on mango fruit which grow in the fields themselves.

The importance of the food obtained from trees is reflected in the laws and customs of many societies. Women, for example, often have the right to utilize breadfruit in the Pacific area even though the tree itself is the province of men, who use it as a source of wood for furniture and canoes. In Nigeria, women may have rights to the kernel but not to the oil of the palm, which is often sold as a cash crop.

Because women are aware of the utility of trees on the homestead, they take good care to plant and maintain them. In many if not most rural societies, it is only the women who have accumulated the traditional knowledge about the foods and other household products that trees can supply. A survey in Sierra Leone has revealed, for example, that women could name thirty-one products that they gathered or made from the nearby bush, while men named only eight.

TREES FOR FUEL

A full granary is no guarantee against famine. Without fuel to cook with, as the women of the Sahel know well, there may be nothing to eat.

Fuelling and tending the household fire has always been women's work. So has the much harder job of collecting and transporting the fuel. One study has shown that in Nepal women and girls together collect 84 per cent of the fuel. Since in many countries fuelwood comprises 80 or 90 per cent of all the wood consumed, this implies

The effects of fuelwood shortages

A survey in eight villages in north-eastern Thailand, where deforestation is becoming severe, has revealed how fuel shortages affect Thai village life. As wood becomes increasingly scarce, women can no longer select the size and types of wood they prefer. Roots and stumps previously left in the fields for coppicing are removed for fuel, and fresh branches are cut from healthy trees (even taboo ones). The weight of fuel used for cooking tends not to diminish, unlike the quality of the fuel, which drops from choice hardwoods to softwoods, and then to agricultural residues such as cassava stems, coconut shells and dried pods. Collecting enough fuelwood thus becomes more time consuming, adding to women's work.

Fuelwood shortages can affect incomes
In north-east Thailand, the best fuelwood is reserved for use in connection with silk-making, which requires accurately controlled temperatures. As select fuels become scarce, women may lose an important source of income. Salt-making, which requires hours of boiling, tends to die out as fuelwood becomes increasingly scarce.

Fuelwood priorities are culturally specific
Night fires that are lit for the buffalo under the house – to keep off the chill and insects – may consume two or three times as much fuel as fires used for cooking. But these fires are maintained even when fuelwood is scarce.

Fuelwood shortages change rituals
A traditional ritual after childbirth is maintaining a comforting fire to warm the mother for a number of days. However, the length of time for which this fire is lit is drastically reduced when fuel is scarce.

that women locate and fetch well over half of all the wood extracted from trees and forests.

Collecting and transporting fuelwood has always been arduous. Fuelwood shortages, though worse today than ever before, are not new: in 1795, a European explorer in what is now the Niger noticed that all wood had been stripped within three kilometres of the city of Kaarta. Today women have to walk much further than three kilometres to collect their fuelwood, and fuelwood for large towns and cities often now comes from 100 km away. The fuelwood shortage in Bangladesh, for example, is so severe that rural women and children spend an average of three to five hours a day gathering and transporting fuel.

Women have acquired an intimate, practical knowledge of the suitability of different tree species for cooking. They know which trees burn slowly and which fast, which smoke and which kindle easily.

The extent of this knowledge is often surprising. In Burkina Faso, for example, women who joined a discussion about what tree species to plant in a forestry project spoke authoritatively about a certain variety of eucalyptus. They knew that burning its leaves kept away mosquitos and that boiling them produced a broth useful for treating colds. They admitted that because the eucalyptus thrives even under arid conditions, and is not preferred by animals for fodder, it might seem useful for fuelwood plantations. But they pointed out that no part of the tree could be eaten by people or domestic stock. They said they found its wood difficult and time-consuming to cut. Though light, it was also sticky. They disliked its fierce burning qualities caused by the presence of an oil in the tree which made its wood burn hot and fast – making it unsuitable for the long, slow cooking needed for most local dishes. And they complained that its smoke gave food a menthol flavour and damaged the eyes. When the tree was planted in gardens or fields, they claimed that it damaged other plants and poisoned the soil.

One of the common misconceptions is that women collect fuelwood simply for cooking. In fact, the homestead fire provides many other benefits. Drinking water is boiled and washing water is warmed on the fire, while fish and meat are smoked above it. The fire provides light at night, and heat to dry a wet harvest. It may also be used to cure tobacco, boil water to extract natural medicines from leaves and bark, and make dyes. The smoke from fires is used to keep insects away. In some countries, household fires are used to keep livestock warm on chilly nights (a use which, in some Thai hill villages, consumes more fuelwood than cooking – see box). Fires also have many social and ritual uses, particularly as the focal centre for evening conversations. In India, the practice of cremation, for example, consumes large amounts of fuelwood.

Thus the fuelwood women collect and transport has many functions. When it becomes short, much more than the family meal is threatened: the basis of village life is altered.

TREES FOR FODDER

Women keep domestic animals in most societies. In Nepal they are responsible for finding fodder for the buffalo – a massive job, because each animal can consume up to 40 tonnes of grass and leaves a year. Elsewhere women keep poultry, goats, pigs, rabbits and other small stock that play an important role in family nutrition, providing additional protein-rich foods such as meat and milk (and sometimes agricultural draught labour as well). In the western highlands of Costa Rica, women keep pigs which feed largely on garden produce, indigenous fruits and other tree products. Some 75 per cent of women keep goats in Egypt and Jordan, and in many of the Sahel countries most of the goats (though rarely the cattle) are kept by women.

In many countries, trees are not valued primarily – as might be thought – for the fuel they provide. A survey in the White Nile Province of the Sudan, for example, found that fodder was the most prized tree product. Shade came second, fuel and poles only third.

Trees are especially valuable as a source of fodder because they can often provide it when other sources are scarce – typically at the end of a dry season or the beginning of a wet one. *Acacia albida*, which is grown in many parts of Africa in or around cultivated fields, scores on both counts. It produces pods late in the dry season, and drops its leaves early in the wet one. As a result, it does not shade crops at the critical stage of their growth yet it provides sustenance for animals when little else is available. In areas where fodder collection is the responsibility of women, such trees play a critical role. The subtle effects all this may have on food production are only beginning to be appreciated. Better fodder means stronger draught animals, and better cultivated land. Crops also benefit from the humus provided by fallen leaves and pods, and the nitrogen that leguminous trees make available to the soil.

At critical times in the agricultural year, fodder trees are invaluable. In the semi-arid zones of Kenya, pigeon peas (*Cajanus canan*), a woody perennial crop, provide both fuelwood and fodder during the critical first two weeks of planting. While men may have the time to graze stock on relatively distant common land, fodder trees grown close to the homestead enable women to raise additional livestock. In the Himalayas, such trees are reserved for use during times of peak labour demand such as rice transplanting.

TREES FOR THE HOUSEHOLD

Women rely on the presence of trees to maintain many parts of their households. While men are usually – though not always – responsible for house construction, it is nearly always the woman's job to carry out minor repairs. Trees provide nearly all that is needed: poles for buildings and sheds, leaves for thatch, canes and stems for wattle, and fibres for twine.

Many of the items that women use in and around the house – spoons, brushes, bowls, mortars and pestles – are made from nearby trees that may be raised specially for that purpose. Fencing within the homestead, vital to protect gardens if small domestic stock are kept, is either made from brushwood or planted as a living fence which may also be productive in its own right. Gathering, building and repairing fencing around household compounds is often women's responsibility and is another major use of wood.

Of the many other products provided by trees, dyes and medicines are particularly important. The bark of many different trees provides a range of colours for dyeing clothes, though often only after prolonged boiling to extract and concentrate the natural pigments. And in many remote areas, medicines extracted from trees and forest plants are still the only form of treatment readily available. In India, for example, the tendu tree (*Diospyros melanoxylon*) has an astringent bark used to treat diarrhoea and dyspepsia. Its dried flowers are also claimed to be effective for the treatment of several urinary, blood and skin diseases.

Trees provide many hundreds of medicines widely used for the treatment of disease. In nearly all traditional societies, medicine is practised by women. It is often considered a domestic craft, knowledge of which is handed down from mother to daughter.

Another household use of trees – one that merits special mention – is shade. The importance of shade has been trivialized or ignored in many accounts of the roles of trees. In fact, the shade that trees provide round the homestead allows households to work and live under conditions that would otherwise prove intolerable. Trees in fields give shade to small children while mothers transplant or weed. Because of this, and for aesthetic reasons, women regularly plant trees around their houses and compounds, and in the fields in which they work.

TREES FOR INCOME

Small-scale, forest-based enterprises, such as the collection and processing of raw materials into useful products, are a major source of income for the poor, and especially for rural women, including those from landless families.

The forest provides many materials that with care, skill and time can be turned into useful products – rattan canes for making furniture, fibres to make nets, ropes and mats, bamboo for basketry, gums and resins, and leaves for making cigarette wrappings (the harvesting of tendu leaves for the latter in India is estimated to employ nearly 600,000 women and children (see box).

In India, in the early 1970s, small-scale, forest-based enterprises provided some 25 per cent of total forest production, more than 60 per cent of forest-based exports, and were responsible for about 1.6 million of the 2.3 million jobs in the forestry sector

The beedi industry: exploitation of the poor

The beedi is a small, cheap cigarette made from tendu leaves wrapped round a small amount of tobacco, sewn up with thread and baked. In India alone, some 2.5 million people were involved in beedi-making in the mid 1970s – and there are probably more now.

About 90 per cent of beedi producers are landless women, mostly working from home, and mostly working long hours – typically, seven hours a day for 285 days a year. Beedi production is one of the few sources of income for these women, since it requires only their labour.

In spite of the income earned from beedi-making, most beedi producers live in extreme poverty: regulations passed to improve working conditions have proved impossible to enforce.

The beedi industry encompasses not only those who make the cigarettes but also those who collect the leaves. More than 350,000 tonnes of leaves are harvested annually by some 600,000 women and children. Many women illegally harvest tendu leaves which are sold to traders who commission the beedi-making and make large profits.

Attempts by the forestry service in Bihar to cut out the middlemen led to bloodshed: riots ensued, forestry offices were burnt to the ground and people killed.

Tendu harvesting and beedi-making are two examples of forest-based, small scale enterprises that benefit millions of Asian women. Improving conditions for these women will, however, be difficult because of the informal nature of the business. The beedi industry provides an opportunity to develop forest policies that benefit poor rural women by providing better access to raw materials and markets.

as a whole. Even these statistics are undoubtedly underestimated because accurate accounts are seldom kept for small enterprises, many of which employ women exclusively. A survey in the Fayoum province of Egypt, for example, showed that 48 per cent of the women there worked in minor forest industries of one kind or another. However, employment in these enterprises is generally on a part-time or seasonal basis, and the wages are low. For women with few ways of earning money, the forest and its products are often the best option.

Because scarcity has so raised the price of fuelwood and charcoal, many women now add to their incomes by selling fuel they gather for others. In a survey of fourteen villages in Himachal Pradesh, India, 70 per cent of the women travelled more than 6 km a day to collect fuelwood for sale or their own use. In Manipur, of a hundred women surveyed, two-thirds collected minor forest products as their only source of income.

The advantages of all these activities are that the raw material is accessible, the work is seasonal and flexible – and can therefore be fitted in with the agricultural season and daily chores – and initial investment is low. For many women, especially those in landless families or without access to common land, the collection of forest products, and fashioning them into saleable commodities, provide the only form of cash income they have.

COMPLEMENTARY USES

Women and men make very different uses of forest resources – even, in many cases, of single species of tree. The uses made of palm trees in Pananao, in the Central Mountains of Dominica, illustrate the different, and sometimes conflicting, roles played by women and men in the exploitation of an important resource.

In Pananao, the control of, responsibility for, and labour involved in exploiting the palm tree vary according to the parts of the tree being used; men use the wood for construction, women use the fibre in handicrafts, and both men and women use the tree's products for animal fodder. Furthermore, the division of control, responsibility and labour shifts with place and activity: near the homestead, only women are involved and on pasture land men exercise all three functions exclusively but for the collection of fuelwood: the divisions are mixed on cropland, where women contribute labour, and on forest 'remnants' – areas of previously overexploited forest – where women are given responsibility for the trees and provide the labour, but men have control of the resource.

However, women control all processing activities even though they do not manage the source areas of the raw materials they need, many of which come from the men's fields, pastures and woodlands. As a result, cassava-bread enterprises have been curtailed by a shortage of fuelwood, and women's handicrafts suffer from a shortage of materials (palm fronds) when men fell the palms for cash.

Forestry projects must therefore analyse the roles played by men and women in the exploitation of forest products if the interests of all groups of users are to be met.

A DEEPENING CRISIS

Events have conspired to deprive women of the relatively easy access they have had to tree products. The problem is not simply environmental: it also reflects the orientation of current development programmes towards cash economies, and widespread failures to understand the real nature of household economies. At the same time, the introduction of new technologies can undermine many of the small-scale forest industries that provide women with at least some cash income.

The ways in which women traditionally use forest resources are becoming increasingly unviable. There are four main reasons for this, each of which has a cumulative, negative impact on the lifestyle of rural women.

1. In many areas, traditionally useful multipurpose tree species are becoming increasingly scarce as desertification and deforestation take their toll. Women therefore have longer to walk to collect fuelwood and other forest products, and this adds further hours to their already overlong working days.

2. As more and more men find employment in the towns and cities, women are forced to carry out jobs previously done by men. This leaves little time for the lengthy business of collecting and processing forest products, however important they many be to the family economy.
3. New technologies are changing land use, reducing the availability of minor forest products that women have traditionally used as a source of additional income. These technologies are frequently introduced without providing women with other income-earning alternatives.
4. Development projects often improve conditions for the men, leaving women with as much, or even more, to do than before.

These four factors need to be considered by planners if they are to help restore the balance between women's needs and the forest and tree resources available to them. Each includes issues related to both poverty and gender.

THE EFFECTS OF RESOURCE DEPLETION

Conventional statistics on the rate of deforestation, or the speed at which desertification is proceeding, mean little to most rural women. The reality of their daily life is the long walk required to fetch fuel and water. As scrubland becomes depleted and the environment deteriorates, and as increasing numbers of people compete for diminishing resources, women find it more and more difficult to collect enough fuelwood in the time available to them.

They are then faced with several alternatives. The first is to use inferior wood for cooking. Softwoods may be substituted for hardwoods, and smaller and less convenient sizes for those normally used. This makes cooking more difficult and more time-consuming. It may also bring about changes in cooking methods, and subsequent changes in the nutritional values of the foods eaten.

The second – and increasingly common – solution is to cook less often. Where once the family could expect two or even three hot meals a day, this is first reduced to one a day and then – as in some parts of West Africa and many areas of the Andes – to one every other day. By this time, family levels of nutrition have usually fallen substantially because many of the staple foods consumed in rural households cannot be easily digested without prolonged cooking. Traditional diets have to be changed, and more and more raw foods introduced into the menu. In the peanut basin of Senegal, women are having to serve water mixed with raw millet flour in place of the cooked grain. In Guatemala, many families can no longer find enough fuel for the lengthy cooking required for their traditional staple of beans.

In the short term, raw food and unboiled water lead frequently to higher levels of disease. In the long term, cooking methods or food substitutions become adapted to the fuels available. Some examples of these adaptive strategies include fermenting beans before cooking to save on cooking time, and substituting less nutritious but quickly cooked foods for more nutritious ones that take longer to cook. The effects of these substitutions on nutrition are only beginning to be examined.

Factors such as length of cooking time have often been ignored in otherwise sound development plans – such as one in Burkino Faso which introduced soya beans into the diet. Many women refused to accept them, however, because they took longer to cook than the traditional cow peas. Throughout the Sahel, rice is increasingly favoured over millet because it is easier to prepare and quicker to cook. But the substitution of imported foods for traditional local crops has played havoc with many African economies and with household food security.

A third solution is to supplement fuelwood supplies with agricultural residues such as cassava stalks and dung. Where fuelwood is in very short supply, these materials become the main fuels of the household. Cooking with them is usually more difficult than with wood, and always requires a far greater bulk of material to be collected, moved and then burnt. Some 800 million people now rely on residues for at least some of their energy needs, and the implications for soil fertility and erosion are serious.

Agricultural wastes are an important form of fertilizer, providing the soil with both humus and inorganic nutrients. If they are burnt in the household, the soil is normally deprived of their fertilizing effect, and becomes impoverished. Lack of humus leads to instability, and wind and water erosion are increased. Lack of fertility means that farmers must cultivate even larger areas of land to provide the quantities of produce their families require.

Severe fuelwood shortages often force women to purchase some of their fuel, usually from trade suppliers. By this time women have in effect lost control of their fuel supply because they have no access to the carts, animals and lorries necessary to turn fuelwood collection from a subsistence activity into a business. Furthermore, they have an added living expense – one that has provoked the West African saying: "It costs as much to cook the rice as it does to fill the bowl".

Resource depletion affects more than fuelwood collection. In the Niger, a whole new market has opened up for the purchase of items that women used to collect for nothing in the nearby forest. In Nepal, where women traditionally gather fodder for their livestock, shortage of trees has made the job almost impossible. When domestic animals have to be given up for lack of fodder – as they have in parts of both Burkina Faso and Mali – another item of food disappears from the subsistence economy, and another source of income disappears from the range of possibilities available to rural women.

Because the impact of forest depletion is felt so severely by women, they are usually anxious to participate in any decisions that are made about what new tree species are to be planted, and where. Women can thus provide an important input to planning. The diagram shows how much activity is crammed into the daily life of a woman living in a small village in Sierra Leone – and in a part of the country where shortages are not as severe as elsewhere in Africa. Nearly all the activities described were carried out while the woman tended her small children. Women in the village had several specific complaints about their lifestyles:

- trees and bushes they needed were becoming difficult to find because of land clearance;
- types of fuelwood needed for cooking special dishes were becoming scarce;
- fish were becoming more difficult to catch because the local pond was silting up;

- the quality of stream water was deteriorating;
- too many rodents in the fields and gardens, probably because predators from the forest were disappearing;
- garden soils becoming "weak" due to overuse, and increasing areas of land needed to feed one family;
- lack of time because fishing, gardening and collecting were taking more time; and
- lack of money because of lack of time to earn even small amounts.

CHANGES IN FAMILY STRUCTURE

One reason why rural women work harder than ever before is that they have increased responsibilities. More and more women are now either legally, or in practice, the heads of their households. There are many reasons for this. Sometimes it is a question of choice, since marriage can confine women to the subsistence economy and provides men with almost total control of cash income. Sometimes it is the result of desertification, divorce or abandonment. But the most common reason is migration. Men are away from home more frequently and for longer periods than they used to be. They go to seek work in the cities, in the mines, on the plantations, and in other countries where the rewards may be – or may appear to be – greater. As a result, at least one-third of all households are now formally headed by women. In one study of seventy-three countries, the country with the smallest proportion of female-headed households was Kuwait, with 10 per cent. The highest was Panama, with 40 per cent. A different study in Kenya, however, showed that 60 per cent of rural households were either headed or managed by women. Overall, the proportion of households where a women is in practice, is not in law, a household head is far higher than even one-third. In all these households, women have to take on jobs that were formerly performed by men. But other changes are occurring as well.

Traditionally, work roles are similar in many societies. Men clear land, turn the soil, hunt and fish, and do some of the planting. Women do the rest – and the rest involves much more than looking after the family. In most societies, women also plant, weed, harvest, carry the crops, fuelwood and fodder home, store them and market the excess. But this division of labour is changing. As cash economies replace subsistence ones, men have less and less to do with food production. Worldwide, women now produce more than 50 per cent of all the food that is grown; in Africa, they produce about 80 per cent. In some areas, large portions of this food come from trees.

A recent survey in Swaziland found that 59 per cent of the ploughing was now being done by women. In some places, the

Sierra Leone: one woman's day

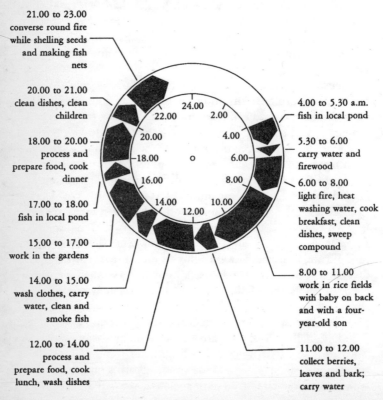

21.00 to 23.00 converse round fire while shelling seeds and making fish nets

20.00 to 21.00 clean dishes, clean children

18.00 to 20.00 process and prepare food, cook dinner

17.00 to 18.00 fish in local pond

15.00 to 17.00 work in the gardens

14.00 to 15.00 wash clothes, carry water, clean and smoke fish

12.00 to 14.00 process and prepare food, cook lunch, wash dishes

4.00 to 5.30 a.m. fish in local pond

5.30 to 6.00 carry water and firewood

6.00 to 8.00 light fire, heat washing water, cook breakfast, clean dishes, sweep compound

8.00 to 11.00 work in rice fields with baby on back and with a four-year-old son

11.00 to 12.00 collect berries, leaves and bark; carry water

woman's workload has increased so much that she cannot cope without more help from her daughters. The two obvious responses are to increase family size so that more labour becomes available, or to take daughters away from school.

One of the major problems with the changing division of labour is that women gain new responsibilities but not the rights that should go with them. Many men now spend so long earning money away from the farm that they are sometimes absent for years on end. Legally, however, they are still the heads of household. The wife has neither title to the land, nor ownership of the cattle she tends. She can use neither as collateral for loans to buy the seed or fertilizer she needs. Frequently, she cannot change land use or adopt new agroforestry practices without permission from her absent husband. There is therefore a need for institutional support for women in their new roles as household heads and managers.

THE EFFECTS OF NEW TECHNOLOGIES

Rural women are one of the last groups in society to benefit from modernization and the introduction of new technology. These are usually targeted at a cash economy rather than the household economy. New agricultural technologies often make life even harder for women. When a male head of household is given credit to buy a cultivator, or a share in a tractor, he soon begins to cultivate more land. His wife and daughters must then weed a larger area in the same time. When new, fast-growing "improved" tree species are introduced, they usually provide a cash crop, often at the expense of the multipurpose species that are used by women for food and fodder production, and to provide a source of income.

Modernization can also be a mixed blessing for women in the forest itself. In timber-rich Borneo, men and women have traditionally worked at wood-cutting as family teams. When heavy chain saws were introduced to improve productivity, women were effectively excluded from an activity that had valuable social as well as fiscal functions.

There is a need to consider the effects that the introduction of a technology may have on poverty itself, and on the respective roles and incomes of both men and women. New technologies, focused specifically on women's needs, are urgently needed. For example, shea butter is the major cooking oil used in many semi-arid areas of Africa. It is processed from the nut of the tree *Butyrospermum parkii* by women who sell the surplus. The process, however, requires heating and prolonged whipping. Women have often requested labour- and energy-saving technologies for the job, but these have yet to be developed.

LOSING OUT ON DEVELOPMENT

In many rural areas, man are the winners in development projects and women the losers. Development experts who plan schemes to improve the lifestyles or increase the incomes of village communities have in the past rarely analysed the gender issues involved. Yet such issues are fundamental to integrated rural development.

When land resources are scarce, plans to maximise production in one area may reduce production in others. Because the things women produce – and particularly those they produce from forest resources – are rarely counted in official statistics, they are ignored. Cash crops are often the foci of forestry development. When more land is devoted to timber or pulp, it has to come from somewhere. Usually, it comes from areas of so-called "useless" scrub. far from being useless, it is these areas on which rural women depend for suppliers of additional food such as fruit and nuts, for medicines, for fodder, and for raw materials for the household.

The ways in which women are affected by unintended side-effects of development projects are often subtle. In the Niger, for example, a highly "successful" windbreak project succeeded in raising crops between the rows of newly planted trees, but women's incomes actually fell as a result of the project. Only later was it realized that women used to keep small ruminants in the areas involved and had given up doing so after they had been fined for allowing their animals to stray into the newly planted areas.

Woodlot projects can also be a mixed blessing for rural women. Their need is for multipurpose trees close to the homestead. Development experts often plan woodlots on the basis of a single species with either good fuelwood or timber characteristics. Men grow and guard the trees, and often sell some of the produce for their own benefit, in effect displacing the women who previously gathered and possibly sold many different forest products from the same area.

New technologies, and the development projects that lie behind them, often improve conditions for the men but leave women with as much – or even more – to do as before.

While the crisis of women and forest resources worsens, some encouragement can be taken from the fact that more is now beginning to be done about it, as the remainder of this chapter makes clear. Two major themes are apparent. In the first, women themselves, either individually or with help from other women and men, have taken up the fight to protect their rights and their resources.

Planners, too, have become more aware of the importance of gender issues in project development and, conversely, of the contribution that women, with their special knowledge of forest resources, can make.

IMPLICATIONS FOR DEVELOPMENT

The time has come to help restore the precarious balance between women and forest resources. While this can often be done by simple changes to development projects, it also requires high-level policy support. It is increasingly obvious that the participation of women in forestry projects is crucial to their success. Foresters and planners must consider women as well as men in their plans for forestry development.

THE ROLE OF WOMEN IN FORESTRY PROJECTS

Women have important roles to play in all phases of a forestry project, either as a separate group or as part of the community. Their inputs are necessary from the stage of problem identification right through to implementation and evaluation. More than twenty years ago, for example, when the taungya system of planting crops between rows of saplings was being encouraged in Ghana, foresters soon recognized that the role of women was critical, for it was they who traditionally grew garden crops. Foresters in Ghana now have a long history of successful collaboration with women.

Projects specifically for women, as well as joint male–female projects, are justifiable, depending on the circumstances. If an activity is traditionally carried out by men, but is taken over and improved by women as part of a project, the women often lose their new role to the men when the project ends. Special care is therefore needed to ensure that women who help plan and execute projects play sustained roles in implementation and receive due benefits from them. One of the most important ways of seeing this is to design projects that provide benefits for both men and women. This is an important reason for avoiding projects in which only women can benefit. Such projects, after all, may be just as invidious as those that are planned by men for men, and deny women any control of the project or benefit from it.

There are, however, some circumstances in which projects designed specifically and exclusively to benefit women appear justified:

- when there are strong taboos against unrelated males and females together;
- where the effects of past discrimination need to be overcome;
- where many or most households are headed by women;
- where women specialize in tasks that could be made more productive with outside help; and
- where women request a measure of self-reliance to avoid conflict or competition with men.

One of the encouraging factors for those who plan forestry projects with identified benefits for women is that women generally have the most to gain. The potential advantages are therefore high.

The advantages of including both men and women in projects became clear in the Cameroon, for example, when men destroyed fences erected round village woodlots; the women, who needed the wood, later helped to repair the fences and convinced the men to accept the project. In Guinea, women have requested projects in which men and women plant trees together. The women felt that if only women were involved men would resent the planting if meals were delayed or women were preoccupied with the project.

The segregation of activities by gender does not have to restrict women to subsistence-level projects. In the Philippines, women are successfully participating in schemes to grow trees as cash crops. In the Republic of Korea and in Senegal, women have banded together to grow seedlings for sale.

Planners are just beginning to appreciate the contribution women can make to forestry development. Women possess a unique indigenous knowledge about the tree species they utilize that can be usefully incorporated into future forest-management strategies. For example, local women who accompanied foresters and extension agents on a field trip in Kenya were able to identify more than twenty species of woody shrubs and plants that were unfamiliar to the rest of the party. Sharing this knowledge with foresters creates the potential for better resource use.

Although women can, and should, play a strong role in forest development, this is not always easy; there are still constraints to their full participation.

CONSTRAINTS TO PARTICIPATION

The factors that militate against women participating fully in forestry projects can be succinctly summarized: women are short of land, time and money; they are often poorly organized, have restricted access to political power, and a limited ability to influence decision-makers; they are more often illiterate than men and have no collateral to offer for credit; and they are restricted in the jobs they are allowed to do and the distances they are allowed to travel.

In a land-hungry world, some of the factors that prevent women from participating in projects are similar to those that exclude men. One of the key issues is land tenure. Because trees grow slowly, few farmers are prepared to plant trees unless they are sure they will enjoy the benefits. They need secure tenure to land and trees. If this is often a problem for men, it is nearly always so for women. Furthermore, legislation to secure tenure often makes things worse for women. A prevalent, but mistaken, attitude has been that if you give to the men, you give to the women. Examples of this attitude have been documented in The Gambia and Kenya, where women who held traditional ownership of land lost it when project adjudicators legally allocated land to male heads of households or to male relatives of female heads of household. Women were left with the traditional responsibilities but no legal rights to the land they farmed. Women without legal rights to land have no collateral to offer for loans to buy equipment, seeds or fertilizer – all of which they need.

Land tenure is, in fact, only one aspect of a general problem of women's rights that can have major effects on the execution of forestry projects. People who have no land have nowhere to plant trees. But more than that, women who have no rights to use certain trees – as is common in many societies – have no incentive to plant them. And women who are forbidden by custom to plant trees have little chance to participate in forestry projects, even those that could provide them with substantial benefits.

If women are to participate in tree-planting projects, they must also have the time. They rarely do. In fact, the more women might benefit from such a project, the less they are likely to have the time to do so. For example, collection of fodder has become immensely time-consuming for women in Nepalese hill villages, but it has sometimes proved hard to persuade them to plant fodder trees. The main reason turns out to be that the women are often too busy collecting fodder to spare the time. A survey showed that on average women in these villages work 10.81 hours a day, compared to 7.51 hours worked by their husbands.

Lack of mobility is another drawback to participation. In many societies, women do not enjoy the same freedom to travel as men, or are not allowed to work away from home. Often women are anxious to lift these restrictions which now appear outmoded to them, however socially useful they may once have been. Experience also shows that traditions of this kind often reflect idealized behaviour rather than what people really do. Poorer women, in any case, have learnt to put survival above theoretical restrictions about the roles they should play in society.

In some cases, simple common sense can resolve the issue. In Kenya, women refused to partake in a honey-producing project

Eight steps to restoring the balance

In developing community forestry, policy-makers should:

1 **EXPLORE** gender issues through two-way communication — with rural women, recognizing that the needs of men and of women may not be the same, and that the impact of projects on them may therefore be different

2 **INVESTIGATE** the customs, taboos and time constraints — that women face, realizing that knowledge and common sense can go a long way to overcoming these constraints

3 **PROMOTE** the role that women do and can play in forestry activities — at each level, and analyse the ways in which projects either include or exclude them

4 **EXCHANGE** information with individuals at every level — with local women on forestry activities, with practitioners on involving women in forestry, with policy-makers on women's roles in forestry

5 **SUPPORT** women's groups and encourage the formation of new ones — that help women gain access to decision-making and the political process, and strengthen women's support for one another

6 **WORK** together to provide access to land and trees — recognizing customary and traditional women's holdings, ensuring women are included where land is privatized, and seeking creative solutions for landless women

7 **COLLABORATE** to make credit and income available to women — either individually, or through women's groups

8 **CONSULT** with women before introducing new technologies or species — ensuring that women's needs have been considered, and the impact of new techniques or trees on women's lives have been evaluated

because the hives were in trees, and tree-climbing was taboo for women. Lowering the hives solved the problem. In the Sudan, the constraint of mobility was overcome by moving nurseries into the women's compounds. A solution to problems of communication between male project staff and women's groups can be resolved by ensuring that women staff are hired for the project. While not all constraints to women's participation are so easily resolved, policy measures can go a long way to help.

EVOLVING FUTURE POLICIES

Sensible policies can overcome some constraints. The first requirement is that women must be specifically (though rarely exclusively) targeted when projects are being formulated. The fundamental need is to evaluate a project's potential impact on – and expected benefits to – both men and women separately. Gender issues need careful analysis if unintended effects on either sex are to be avoided.

Preliminary research may be needed to establish exactly how a project is likely to affect women. Such things are not always obvious. A common mistake in the past, for example, has been to introduce new crops or products that require heat-processing or excessive drying. These innovations may well increase men's incomes, but only at the expense of making much arduous work for the women who have to collect the extra fuelwood.

Enquiries need to be made into the needs, interests, talents and desire for participation of the women in communities to be affected by forestry projects. In effect, this means involving women in project design as well as project execution. Doing so can automatically eliminate some of the less desirable practices of the past in which, for example, projects have specifically planned to employ large numbers of women in nurseries – but only because they could be paid less than the men.

Another fundamental issue that will require further analysis in the future concerns the role of women in the cash economy. Because women have traditionally operated in the subsistence sector, it is tempting to design projects to assist them only in their traditional roles. In fact, women urgently need to be brought more fully into the cash economy, and to be provided with credit and security of land tenure on an equal basis with men.

If means can be found to enable women to participate, if sufficient numbers of sensitive professionals can be found to make the initial contacts and carry out preliminary research, and if gender issues are specifically identified early on in project planning, future forestry projects could break much more new ground.

In the process, both rural women and professional foresters could gain a great deal. Enabling women to benefit more fully from forest resources is likely to prove one of the most rewarding and environmentally benign ways of fighting rural poverty.

SOURCES

The ideas expressed in this chapter rely heavily on the writings and research of Robert Chambers, Carol Colfer, Ruth Dixon, Louise Fortmann, Marilyn Hoskins, Shobita Jain, Richard Longhurst, Augusta Molnar, John Raintree, Dianne Rouchleau and Mercedes Wiff, to whom acknowledgement is gratefully made. None of these authors, however, is responsible for the use that has been made of their work here. D'Arcy Davis Case also provided editorial wisdom and inspiration.

The literature on women and forest products is widely scattered. The references that follow are not of source material but of more general publications that treat the subject in a broad context.

REFERENCES

Carr, Marilyn, *Appropriate Technology for Women: Two essays* (London: Intermediate Technology Development Group, 1982).

ESCAP, *Report of the Expert Group Meeting on Women and Forest Industries* (Bangkok: ESCAP, 1980).

FAO, Follow-up to WCARRD: The role of women in agricultural production (Rome: FAO Committee on Agriculture, 1982).

FAO, *Forests, Trees and People* (Rome: FAO, 1985, Forestry Topics No. 2).

FAO, *Tree Growing by Rural People* (Rome: FAO, 1985, FAO Forestry Paper No. 64).

91

FAO, *Wood for Energy* (Rome: FAO, 1983, Forestry Topics No. 1).

Hoskins, Marilyn, *Household Level Appropriate Technologies for Women* (Washington, DC: US Agency for International Development, Office of Women in Development, 1981).

Hoskins, Marilyn, *Rural Women, Forest Outputs and Forestry Projects* (Rome: FAO, 1983).

Hoskins, Marilyn, *Women in Forestry for Local Community Development* (Washington, DC: US Agency for International Development, Office of Women in Development, 1979).

Rouchleau, Dianne E, "The User Perspective and the Agroforestry Research and Action Agenda", in Golz, Henry (ed.), *Agroforestry* (Dordrecht, the Netherlands: Martinus Nijhoff/Dr W. Junk Publishers, 1987).

Scott, G., *Forestry Projects and Women* (Washington, DC: World Bank, 1980).

Tinker, Irene, *Women, Energy and Development* (Washington, DC: Equity Policy Center, 1982).

"Women in Forestry", *Unasylva*, vol. 36, no. 146, 1984/4 (Rome: FAO).

Wood, D.H. *et al*, *The Socio-Economic Context of Firewood Use in Small Rural Communities* (Washington, DC: US Agency for International Development, 1980).

UNDER THE COOKING POT: THE POLITICAL ECONOMY OF THE DOMESTIC FUEL CRISIS IN RURAL SOUTH ASIA

Bina Agarwal

THE CRISIS

> When we were young we used to go to the forest early in the morning. . . . In a short while we would gather all the fodder and firewood we needed, rest under the shade of some huge tree and then go home. Now, with the going of the trees, everything else has gone too. [A woman in the Uttarakhand hills, India (Bahuguna, 1984:132)]

In the Himalayan foothills of Nepal, a journey to gather firewood and fodder took an hour or two a generation ago – today it takes the whole day (Eckholm, 1975). An observer notes: "Nowhere can there be seen a tree or bush unscarred by axes, knives and browsing domestic animals. The imprint of people searching for fuel and fodder is to be seen everywhere" (Hughart, 1979:28). In Bihar, seven or eight years ago, women of poor rural households could get enough firewood for self-consumption and sale within one and a half to two kilometres – they now trek eight to ten kilometres per day (Bhaduri and Surin, 1980). In some villages of Gujarat where the surrounding forests have been completely denuded, women spend long hours collecting weeds and shrubs and digging out the roots of trees. These do not provide continuous heat and increase cooking time (Nagbrahman and Sambrani, 1983).

Fuel shortages are driving villagers in several regions of South Asia to shift to foods that require less fuel but are of lower nutritional value, or to miss some meals altogether and go hungry (Hughart, 1979). Necessity is also driving people in some areas to shift to food which can be eaten raw but is less nutritious, or to eat partially cooked food (which could be toxic), or to eat cold leftovers (with the danger of food rotting in a tropical climate). This is the human face of the crisis of cooking fuel shortages that is surfacing with growing urgency in rural South Asia.

Today we can no longer associate the problem of hunger only with food sufficiency – it is linked crucially to fuel sufficiency. As one observer aptly put it: "Lack of fuel can be as much a cause of malnutrition as a lack of food" (Poulsen, 1978). This has for generations been part of the conventional wisdom of rural women who have said: "It's not what's in the pot that worries you, but what's under it". But it is a concern that has not permeated beyond rhetoric and piecemeal measures in the development planning of South Asia.

The crucial aspect that needs recognition is the three-way link between the cooking energy crisis, poverty and socioeconomic inequalities. This recognition is necessary not only for appropriately pinpointing the implications of the crisis and its complex causes, but also for understanding why most state-instituted tree-planting and other schemes launched ostensibly to alleviate the crisis have failed so dismally. This chapter seeks to explicate the link. In doing so it also posits the question: can we effectively deal with the cooking energy problem without any measures to reduce existing socioeconomic (especially land-based) inequalities, and without re-examining the development strategies adopted in South Asia?

Table 1 highlights the significance of fuelwood (wood-based fuel, essentially firewood and charcoal) as a source of inanimate energy in South Asia. Existing estimates suggest that much of this is consumed directly as firewood. If we take energy consumption by the rural domestic sector alone, the importance of firewood is greater still. In the hills and desert areas of Northern India, an estimated 67 and 65 per cent respectively of total domestic energy consumed by rural households is from this one source (NCAER, 1981); although the average for Northern India as a whole is lower – 42 per cent – and for Southern India it is 31 per cent (Table 2) Also, over 90 per cent of domestic energy is used for cooking and water-heating in both regions. While the macro-surveys do not give cross-tabulations of the fuel source by end-use, micro-studies for India indicate that in large parts of the country firewood is the single most important cooking fuel – in some villages it provides 100 per cent of cooking energy. More typically, however, in India and in South Asia generally, firewood is supplemented by animal wastes and crop residues, the proportions varying according to the availability of different fuels to the household. Firewood is the preferred fuel, and the substitution of firewood by inferior fuels such as paddy straw, dung or leaves and weeds, usually reflects the household's poor economic status. A Bangladesh field study shows a sharp decrease in the proportionate and absolute daily consumption of firewood per household with farm size (Howes and Jabbar, 1986).

Table 1 Commercial and fuelwood energy consumption in South Asia, 1982

Country	Commercial energy per capita Kg CE	Fuelwood consumption per capita Kg CE	Fuelwood as a % of total energy (commercial and fuelwood)
Bangladesh	49.8	108.5	68.5
India	200.6	96.8	32.5
Nepal	11.2	298.6	96.4
Pakistan	225.8	68.7	23.3
Sri Lanka	121.9	163.8	57.3

Note: CE = coal equivalent
Source: Agarwal 1986a:8-9

In much of rural South Asia, firewood and other domestic fuels such as crop residues and dung are gathered, and seldom purchased. In parts of Nepal and Bangladesh all firewood needs are met by self-collection. In rural North India only an estimated 26 per cent of firewood, 9 per cent of dung and 5 per cent of crop wastes are purchased: for rural South India the percentages are 10, 5 and 5 respectively (NCAER, 1981; ITES 1981). The bulk of

the domestic fuel is gathered by households from their own
resources or from common land and forests, or from the land of
others.

Table 2 Domestic fuel consumption per household by income class,
fuel type and end-use in rural India

Income class Rs/annum	Total domestic energy	Type of fuel				End use			
		Fire-wood	Dung cakes	Crop/ vegetable waste	Char-coal	Other	Cooking	Water heating*	Lighting
Northern India	1,315	551	312	382	8	62	1,203	67	45
(1975–76)	(100)	(42)	(24)	(29)	(1)	(5)	(91)	(5)	(3)
Up to 3,000	953	374	259	276	6	38	868	52	33
	(100)	(39)	(27)	(29)	(1)	(4)	(91)	(5)	(4)
3,001–6,000	1,874	862	394	516	6	96	1,724	87	63
	(100)	(46)	(21)	(28)	(n)	(5)	(92)	(5)	(3)
6,001–9,000	2,323	905	516	810	3	89	2,130	124	69
	(100)	(39)	(22)	(35)	(n)	(4)	(92)	(5)	(3)
Over 9,000	3,136	1,454	516	889	53	224	2,890	137	109
	(100)	(46)	(16)	(28)	(2)	(7)	(92)	(4)	(3)
Southern India	1,562	489	434	554	9	76	915	588	59
(1979–80)	(100)	(31)	(28)	(35)	(1)	(5)	(59)	(38)	(4)
Up to 3,000	1,432	455	368	557	1	51	863	519	50
	(100)	(32)	(26)	(39)	(n)	(4)	(60)	(36)	(4)
3,001–8,000	1,781	549	554	542	22	114	997	711	73
	(100)	(31)	(31)	(30)	(1)	(6)	(56)	(40)	(4)
Over 8,000	2,347	687	593	694	44	329	1,337	843	167
	(100)	(29)	(25)	(30)	(2)	(14)	(57)	(36)	(7)

Notes: Figures are kilograms of coal replacement.
Figures in brackets give the percentage of total energy used; n = negligible
* Figures also include space heating in the case of Northern India.
Source: NCAER 1981:105. 107: ITES 1981:424.425

As asset holdings decline, the dependency on fuel collection from
sources other than one's own increases. Landed rural households
can obtain firewood (often through hired labour) from trees located
on their own land, residues from their crops, and dung from
the cattle they own. The landless, however, have to depend for
firewood and supplementary fuel on forest and common land or

obtain it from other people's land in return for work done. this dependence is clearly brought out in Table 3, covering the semi-arid areas of five Indian States. It is noteworthy that common property resources (CPRs), which are of marginal importance as fuel sources for the larger farmers, provide 66–84 per cent (varying by region) of the domestic fuel and 91–100 per cent of the firewood consumed by small farmer and landless households.

Table 3 Domestic fuel consumption by household economic position and source of fuel in rural India

District/State	Household's economic position	Weekly fuel consumption per household (kg)	Per cent fuel from			
			CPRs	Own Sources		
				Firewood	Dung	Crop residues
Mahbubnagar	Poor (13)	119	84	-	9	8
(Andhra Pradesh)	Others (7)	190	13	26	41	20
Akola	Poor (13)	104	79	-	3	18
(Maharashtra)	Others (7)	185	13	20	24	43
Sholapur	Poor (13)	119	72	2	12	14
(Maharashtra)	Others (7)	205	10	18	34	38
Sabarkantha	Poor (20)	184	66	-	25	9
(Gujarat)	Others (10)	213	8	18	28	46
Raisen	Poor (20)	185	74	9	11	6
(Madhya Pradesh)	Others (10)	219	32	24	29	15

Notes: "Poor" includes agricultural labourer and small farmer (with <2 ha of dry land equivalent) households.

"Others" includes only large farmer households (i.e. the top 20 per cent of landowners in the village).

Figures in brackets give sample size.

CPRs: Common Property Resources.

Source: Jodha, 1986: 1173

The overall dependency of the rural population on self-collection of domestic fuel, and the dependency of the rural poor in particular on common land, leads to significant variations in fuel (and especially firewood) consumption by ecological regions (particularly due to differences in locational availability) and by income class of household within the region. Table 4 clearly brings out these differences. In North India, for instance, the firewood consumed per rural household in the hills is twice as much as in the plains in absolute terms, and almost twice as much in terms of the percentage of total domestic fuel used. Equally striking is the positive relationship between income group and the amount of firewood consumed – consumption decreases consistently as income levels fall in each region. Table 3 provides additional evidence of a clear positive association between all domestic fuel consumed and the household's access to land. In other words, a household's landholding status affects its access not only to food but also to the fuel to cook it, and the greater the concentration of land and cattle ownership, the greater are likely to be the inequalities in access to fuel. Village studies by Briscoe (1979) and Islam (1980) in Bangladesh clearly highlight this. Briscoe found that 89 per cent of all fruit and firewood trees in the village were owned by 16 per cent of the families, who also owned 55 per cent of the cropped land and 46 per cent of the cattle. Islam similarly found that 52.3 per cent of the trees in the six villages he surveyed were owned by 11.4 per cent of the households.

With increasing deforestation and the degradation as well as declining availability of common land, these differences are likely to be strengthened further. Jodha's (1983, 1986) research for India indicates that over the past three decades the area and productivity of CRPs has declined by 26–63 per cent (varying by region) due to the privatization of this land in favour of the larger landed households, forcing the landless and near-landless to depend on decreasing tracts of common land. In addition (as elaborated later) the Green Revolution technology has reduced the availability of crop and animal wastes to the poor in complex ways. Growing urban demands have also accelerated the commercialization of firewood, the prices of which have more than doubled over the last decade in much of South Asia, and increased tenfold over the past two decades in several cities.

Basically, as firewood, crop residues and dung get scarcer and increasingly monetized, those who have no fuel-yielding assets and little purchasing power will tend to get squeezed out. For such households, there can even be a trade-off between fuel and food. For instance, in rural Bangladesh, landless Hindus, who are typically economically and socially the worst off, have to buy firewood during the monsoon when crop residues are not available at the cost of buying food (Briscoe, 1979).

Table 4 Annual consumption of firewood per household by region and income class in rural India

Income class/Region (Rs./year)	Hills Kg CR % TDEC*		Plains Kg CR % TDEC		Desert Kg CR % TDEC		All Regions Kg CR % TDEC	
Northern India	1,103	67	466	36	822	65	551	42
1975–76	(1,656)		(1,275)		(1,271)		(1,315)	
Up to 3,000	926	67	293	32	624	67	374	39
3,001 to 6,000	1,310	65	774	42	1,072	61	862	46
6,001 to 9,000	1,663	59	795	35	1,571	69	905	39
Over 9,000	2,320	82	1,362	43	1,661	65	1,454	46

	Hills		Plains		Coastal		All Regions	
Southern India	549	34	584	34	362	26	489	31
1979–80	(1,612)		(1,728)		(1,367)		(1,562)	z
Up to 3,000	534	36	568	34	294	25	455	32
3,001 to 8,000	571	32	604	33	484	28	549	31
Over 8,000	806	23	1,084	44	412	22	686	29

Notes: CR = Coal replacement: TDEC = Total Domestic Energy Consumption.
  * per cent of firewood energy in TDEC in respective income class and region.
  Figures in brackets give the TDEC for the region as a whole
Sources: NCAER, 1981: 105. 107: ITES, 1981: 424, 426–8

Particularly revealing in this regard is Howes and Jabbar's (1986) study of a sample of Bangladeshi households, which gives information on changes over the past ten years of the average number of *all* meals and *cooked* meals consumed daily by different classes of households (big farmers, owner-cultivators, share-croppers and landless). While the big farmers can still afford three meals (almost all cooked) a day, the small owner-cultivators and sharecroppers have shown a small decrease, and the landless a significant decrease, both in the total number of meals consumed and in the number of cooked meals consumed.

Women in poor households bear the highest burden. As the main gatherers of fuel it is primarily their time and effort that are extended with shortages. Also, they (and female children) face more severe nutritional consequences from such shortages than males because of a systematic bias against them in the distribution of food within the family (Agarwal, 1986b). This unequal distribution and poverty mean, too, that the women are unlikely to get the extra food necessary to make up for the additional energy they expend in fuel collection. Further, as other sources of livelihood are eroded, selling firewood for an income is becoming increasingly common among the poor in many parts of South Asia (especially in eastern India, Nepal and Bangladesh). By one estimate, two to three million rural people in India are so dependent. Most of them are women, earning a meagre Rs.5.50 or so a day for a headload of 20 kg of wood (Agarwal and Deshingkar, 1983).

At the macro-level, by FAO estimates, some 1.4 billion people in rural Asia and the Pacific are likely to be facing an acute scarcity of fuelwood in the year 2000. This includes, in particular, people in India, Pakistan, Nepal and Bangladesh. And within these countries, it will include essentially the poor, especially in the semi-arid regions.

WHAT FACTORS UNDERLIE THE CRISIS?

Impinging on this crisis is a complex set of interrelated issues: (i) the absolute availability of wood for all uses (which depends on the tree resources of the country, barring imports); (ii) the availability of wood for fuel (which depends on the distribution of existing wood supplies between different uses); (iii) the availability of fuelwood to the poor (which depends on the distribution of wood supplies between people). As elaborated below, firewood shortages being faced by the poor today emerge from the particular uses to which forest land and wood resources have been put over the years by specific classes of people, and cannot be traced in any straight-forward way to the gathering of firewood by the poor for their domestic use. Historically, under British rule, there was virtually indiscriminate forest exploitation in India through European and Indian private contractors, especially for the expansion of railways in the mid-nineteenth century and for building ships, bridges, etc., in the inter-World War years. As documented by British observers (see Guha, 1983), large tracts of forests in the Garhwal and Kumaon hills were "felled in even to desolation", often without adequate supervision, so that "thousands of trees were felled which were never removed nor was their removal possible". Vast areas of mountain forest were also given away to selected individuals to set up tea and coffee plantations, in addition to encouraging forest clearance for crop cultivation to augment the colonial government's land revenues. Nepal, while not directly under colonial rule, was strongly influenced and guided by the British Indian Forest Services and experienced considerable intensive felling, especially during the 1920s and 1930s (Bajracharya, 1983).

The cutting of forests for commercial use has continued in the post-colonial period to provide building logs, industrial raw material – especially to the paper manufacturers – fuel to small-scale and cottage industries, etc. Forest land has also been lost due to mining, stone quarrying, agriculture and large river valley projects. According to official statistics for India, between 1951–2 and 1975–6, 4.14 million hectares were deforested – agriculture and river valley projects accounting for 60.2 per cent and 11.6 per cent of this area respectively. However, Forestry Department statistics, even on total forested area, were subsequently shown to be very wide of the mark by National Remote Sensing Agency data. These revealed that in 1972–5, 55.5 million hectares or 16.9 per cent of land, was forested (the official claim being 23 per cent): by 1980–81 it had fallen to 46.4 million hectares or 14.1 per cent – an annual fall of 1.3 million hectares. In fact a good deal of felling continues to be illegal, and no clear-cut estimates yet exist on what proportion of the forests are being cut for which purposes and at what rates.

What is noteworthy, however, is that the use of wood for almost all purposes other than as a domestic fuel in the rural areas requires the cutting down of trees. Firewood, in contrast, can be collected in the form of twigs and fallen branches, which does not lead to tree destruction. And both micro- and macro-studies indicate that this in fact is the form in which firewood is typically gathered. Briscoe finds this in his Bangladesh village study; in Pura village (Karnataka, India) 91 per cent of the firewood is consumed in this form (Ravindranath et al., 1978); and NCAER (1981) estimates that nearly 75 per cent of the firewood used as domestic fuel in rural North India is in the form of twigs and branches. Interestingly, to the extent that *logs* are burnt as domestic fuel, the culprits are noted to be the higher income groups and not the poor.

In short, the link between deforestation (and associated firewood shortages) and domestic firewood consumption by the poor is a tenuous one. And even to the extent that in some areas trees are being cut or the barks of trees being stripped off by the poor to obtain fuel, it must be seen as a *symptom* of the crisis – a reaction of the people who are the worst hit but who cannot be held responsible for having *caused* the crisis.

This becomes even more apparent when we examine what has been happening to the access of the poor to CPRs on the one hand and to forests on the other. Both Jodha's (1983, 1986) work on India (mentioned earlier) and Cernea's (1981) study on the Azad Kashmir area of Pakistan point to the gradual appropriation of CPRs by large farmers. Jodha attributes this largely to the way land-reform programmes in the 1950s and subsequent welfare schemes were implemented: considerable areas of CPRs were demarcated for distribution to the landless, but in practice much of the land so privatized went to the larger farmers. In Rajasthan, for instance, in the villages he surveyed, the landless received only 14–24 per cent (varying by district) of the land distributed – almost all of it of poor quality. And by the time of the survey they had lost control over much of even this – having sold or mortgaged it due to its poor quality and/or the lack of resources to develop it. Hence the collective loss of CPRs by the poor was not made up by their privatized gain. A similar trend of *de facto* appropriation of community land by large farmers in Azad Kashmir is described by Cernea.

Likewise, the history of forest policy in the subcontinent reveals the systematic marginalization and uprooting of tribal populations by various state schemes – such as the settlement of non-tribals on tribal land, and the reservation of forests (in effect barring them from entering areas on which they depended for a livelihood).

As Guha (1983) notes, the Forestry Department was created in India in 1864 under colonial rule and was accompanied by legislation curtailing the previously unlimited rights of users over forest produce, giving the state monopoly rights over land. Various Forest Acts sought to establish that the customary use of forests by the villagers was based not on "rights" but on "privilege" which could be exercised only at the discretion of the local rulers. Large tracts of forest were also fenced off, increasing the population pressure on the remaining land. Practices of shifting agriculture had earlier incorporated long fallows, allowing adequate time for regeneration. Also, the adaptation of tribal communities to population growth took the form of the gradual development of orchards and settled farming alongside swidden. Today increasing numbers are being forced to survive on diminishing tracts of "common" forest which they are then held responsible for destroying. Here the issue is not one of "weaning the tribal population from shifting agriculture" by "careful demonstration of improved methods" and "persuasive means" (see Noval and Polycarpau, 1969) but of the absence of alternative sources of livelihood, and the erosion of community life in which the social and the economic had earlier been closely inter-woven in ways conducive to preserving the environmental balance.

There is also evidence from all over South Asia of the exploitation of tribals by the forest guards (who are usually placed at the lowest rung of the Forestry Service hierarchy). There are examples from different parts of India of guards taking a share of the value of minor forest produce collected by the tribals, of making them work without wages, of collecting regular tributes from them and implicating non-givers in legal cases with the connivance of the local police, of meting out punishments at the smallest transgression into the so-called reserve forests, of levying huge fines (for which no receipt is given) for minor offences, and even of beating tribals mercilessly on the smallest pretext (see Joshi, 1981; Chand and Bezboruah, 1980; Swaminathan, 1982a). Similarly, in the Azad Kashmir region in Pakistan, 50,000 cases of forest offences are noted to be pending in courts, with one family in every six being implicated in a reported offence (Cernea, 1981). In Bangladesh again, a ten-village study revealed numerous cases of harassment of the landless by local police and forest officials (BRAC, 1980:73–6).

Not surprisingly perhaps, today there is noted to be a widespread feeling that the forest officials are "instruments of the government (which is distant and threatening)" and exploiters who take bribes, harass, threaten and extort in the name of unfamiliar laws, and are gradually taking away from the people their natural habitat – namely, the forest (Roy, 1980).

Ninan (1983) attributes the behaviour of guards in the Indian Forestry Service to low salaries ("a guard who polices several lakh rupees' worth of valuable forest is paid only Rs.300 per month"), and to hierarchies in the Service. She emphasizes the need to reduce inequalities in the Service and to crack down on the culture of blatant corruption. How this can be done in a structure built on hierarchies and privilege is a moot question.

Also, corruption is not limited to the guards. A Bangladesh case study documents the illegal cutting of trees on government land by locally powerful timber merchants, with the unofficial co-operation (via bribes) of Forest Officers. The merchants bought plots, situated inside the government forests, from the tribals at very cheap rates; and obtained permits to fell trees on these plots. But this land had few trees, and 90 per cent of the trees they actually cut were on the government land adjacent to their plots (BRAC, 1980). Nath (1968) documents a similar case of the illegal exploitation of government forests and local tribal land by timber merchants in Madhya Pradesh, India. In this context, it is especially pertinent to ask: "For whom are these forests reserved? Protected for whom? Protected from whom?" (Swaminathan, 1982a:344).

Firewood shortages apart, the domestic fuel crisis has been further exacerbated by the adverse effect of the Green Revolution technology on the availability of crop residues and dung to the poor. For instance, shifts in cropping patterns in parts of Bangladesh, with jute being replaced extensively by tubewell-irrigated HYV *boro* rice, has reduced the availability of jute sticks for fuel which formed a significant part of the payment to female hired labour (Howes and Jabbar, 1986). Also, high-yielding dwarf crop varieties relative to traditional varieties give lesser crop residue per unit weight of grain, which is not necessarily made up by higher per acre crop output. Further, in recent years, combine harvesters are becoming increasingly popular among the Indian farmers (as in Punjab and Haryana). These displace labour and leave virtually no crop residues. In contrast, under manual harvesting, employment is higher and labourers are often paid in grain along with the straw or stalks. Again, tubewell irrigation in semi-arid areas (as in Kolar district, Karnataka) has led to a significant drop in the water table, further degrading CPRs. Moreover, in general, with the spread of irrigation it is now more profitable to use dung as manure, leaving less for the labourers to forage as fuel. In fact, by one estimate, between 1963–4 and 1973–4 there has been a decline in the dung burnt as fuel in India, even while dung output in general and that used as manure has increased (Desai, 1980).

Changing production relations in agriculture and the growing scarcity of biomass are also leading to modifications in tenancy contracts: in parts of Bangladesh sharecroppers now have to give the landlord not just half the crop but half the crop residues too (Howes and Jabbar, 1986). Also, with the new agricultural technology, there is a trend in many parts of South Asia towards resumption of land under personal cultivation, with a consequent decline in leased-out land and increasing landlessness. This is forcing increasing numbers to depend on uncertain fuel supplies from diminishing tracts of common resources.

Ultimately, therefore, the distribution of energy resources between uses and users impinges on central aspects of political economy – on the distribution of material wealth and political power between different classes and social groups within the country, which determines *who* gets across to *how much* of a scarce resource, and for *what* purpose.

These aspects of political economy which underlie the domestic fuel crisis facing the poor also overshadow attempts to alleviate it. This emerges clearly from the experience of tree-planting schemes, a very large number of which have been initiated in the past few years by national and international agencies, usually under the banner of a catch-all phrase – "social forestry" – and which are now being promoted as *the* solution to both the firewood crisis and the environmental crisis.

THE EXPERIENCE OF TREE-PLANTING SCHEMES

Tree production can be promoted under individual, government or community management, on private, government or community (belonging jointly to a village or group) land, for commercial, or non-commercial use. "Farm forestry" usually implies individuals growing trees (to sell or for own use) on private land. "Social forestry", on the other hand, implies the planting of trees for meeting the needs (especially of fuel and fodder) of the rural people, usually through the use of government or community land, under government or community management. Such planting when undertaken by the community (typically on village land), is also often termed "community forestry".

In recent years, numerous schemes under all three systems of management and on different types of land, have been launched, many funded by international aid agencies such as FAO, SIDA, the World Bank and USAID. Yet available evaluation studies (some detailed, some impressionistic) indicate that while farm forestry has had a limited success in parts of South Asia, social forestry, with very few exceptions, has been a failure in most places, even in the sense of ensuring the planting and maturing of trees, let alone in providing for the daily needs for fuel, fodder, etc., of the rural poor.

Tree-planting by the government

Many of the schemes where governments have directly taken charge of tree-planting have been introduced in opposition to the wishes of the people rather than with their support. This is especially so where the reservation of degraded forest land for tree-planting has restricted or terminated the rights of farmers, cattle-grazers or hunters to the hitherto "free" produce of the forest. Such reservations have particularly hit tribal communities whose main sustenance has come from the forests for generations. Also the restrictions have usually been imposed from above without the involvement of the local community in the decision.

In some cases, land has been taken over to plant trees solely for commercial purposes. There are several examples of this from India. In Bihar, the Forestry Department sought to replace a mixed forest by a monoculture teak plantation. Not only were the teak trees of no immediate use to the people, but the establishment of the plantation deprived the tribals of existing rights to collect minor forest produce. As a result, the local residents axed many of the teak trees, to deter the extension of the plantations at the cost of their mixed forest (Makhijani, 1979). Again, in Midnapore district (West Bengal), eucalyptus and other commercial varieties are noted to have been forcibly planted by the Forestry Department on plots where the tribals originally grew paddy (*Indian Express*, 1983). In Uttar Pradesh, *sheesham* and *sal* were cut to plant eucalyptus (Dogra, 1984). Likewise in Bastar district (Madhya Pradesh), under a World Bank-funded project, 40,000 hectares of deciduous forest were to be clear-felled to plant tropical pine as raw material for the paper industry. This brought strong resistance from the tribals, leading to a public controversy and the eventual shelving of the scheme (Guha, 1983; D'Monte, 1982).

Problems with government programmes stem not only from the land-use policy of the Forestry Department but also from the attitudes and practices of the Forest Officials who in India (as also elsewhere in Asia) are noted to be typically "tree orientated" and not "people orientated". Hence, even while the officials may accept that community forestry is *for* the people, they are still far from saying that it is *by* the people. They seek to decide what is good for the community rather than letting the community decide what is good for them and helping them to achieve it (Roy, 1980).

In several cases people's own initiatives are found to have been thwarted by forest authorities through lengthy bureaucratic procedures and unhelpful attitudes (UTTAN, 1983; Swaninathan, 1982b). In many others, trees planted by villagers on their private land have been claimed by the government as its property (Sarin, 1980; Romm, 1979). Here the villagers now refuse to plant trees without a written assurance that those planted on their land are their property.

All said, both the protection of existing forests and the government's new tree-planting schemes, far from benefiting the rural poor, have in most cases further deprived them of their existing rights. Essentially, these projects, undertaken in the name of social forestry, provide no guarantee that the benefits will flow to the people, and especially to those who put in the labour. The absence of such a surety also underlies the failure of most of the so-called community forestry schemes, to which I shall now turn.

Community forestry schemes

The assumption in such schemes is that the community will actively participate in tree-planting. Yet, on the one hand, little effort is made by the scheme initiators actively to involve the people in scheme conceptualization and implementation; and, on the other, the unequal pattern of land-ownership and control, and the power structures operating in the village, circumvent voluntary participation by the underprivileged. Consider a project in the Azad Kashmir region of Pakistan, where it was assumed that tree plantations would come up on three types of land: *Shamlat* (community), government and private. Planting on *Shamlat* land was meant to ensure that the main benefits would flow to the small farmers who were in a majority in the community but had little access to firewood; this was also expected to promote direct community participation. Planting on the government land was to demonstrate the benefits of the fast-growing tree species to the farmers, to induce them to plant trees on their own land.

In practice, the project's success lay mainly in its promotion of private tree-planting by the larger farmers. The latter were also willing to invest in the *Shamlat* land, but the smaller farmers were unwilling to do so. Cernea (1981) describes the underlying reasons for the failure of community forestry. While in legal terms *Shamlat* land continues to be considered community land, in reality much of it is operated as private land. Also, the usufruct benefits from the so-called *Shamlat* land accrue to the larger farmers rather than to the community as a group. The *de facto* owners hope to get the land planted at full government expense with no repayment commitment, and also in the process restrict the current rights to fodder and grass which the small farmers enjoy over this land. The latter are thus unwilling to put in labour for planting trees on this land, as not only is the prospect of their getting any benefits low but their limited rights to grazing, etc., are also in danger.

This is in fact a familiar story in the subcontinent, and this *de facto* control by village factions over community land crucially affects village forestry schemes. In both Gujarat and Uttar Pradesh (India), in World Bank-aided forestry projects started in the early 1980s, the village self-help woodlot components have largely failed. A mid-term appraisal report for Gujarat attributed the lack of success to the non-homogeneous nature of the village community, the mistrust in the system regarding its ability to ensure equitable distribution of woodlot output, disputes among farmers on the availability of common land for establishing village woodlots, and so on (World Bank, 1983a).

The clear pointer from these experiences is the particular difficulty, if not impossibility, of successfully implementing such schemes within agrarian structures that are characterized by sharp socioeconomic inequalities. The lesson is reinforced when we examine the few success stories.

In the Indian context, one of the noteworthy cases of successful community mobilization for tree protection and planting – the Chipko movement – comes from the hills of Uttar Pradesh, where 95 per cent of the forest land is owned by the government and managed by the Forestry Department. The movement was mainly sparked off in 1972–3 by the people in Chamoli district protesting against the allotment of vast tracts of ash forest for felling to a sports goods manufacturer, while a local labour co-operative was refused permission to cut a few trees for making agricultural implements for the community. The villagers (including women), mobilized by the co-operative, resorted to *Chipko* (meaning to cling to or embrace the trees), challenging the employees of the sports goods company to axe them first. Since then people in the region have sought to end the contractor system of forest exploitation, demanded a ban on green felling and excessive resin tapping, and agitated for minimum wages for forest labourers. In several instances peaceful protest demonstrations by Chipko activists have led to the cancellation of tree auctions (Dogra, 1984). The campaign is now focused on both tree protection and reforestation. Women in particular, have been at the forefront both in the protest demonstrations and in maintaining vigilance against illegal felling.

The movement has also highlighted the fact that women and men, even of the same class of household, can have different priorities, and that the interests and concerns of the women tend to be much more directly related to ecological preservation. For example, in 1980 a government scheme to cut down a large tract of the Dungari-Paitoli oak forest (in Chamoli district), to establish a potato seed farm and other infrastructure, was strongly and successfully opposed by the local women who resorted to Chipko to save the trees. The scheme was supported by the village men (especially those of the village council) who saw in it the potential for profit. The women, however, argued that forest destruction would take away their main source of fuel, fodder and water, while cash in the men's hands was likely to be frittered away on tobacco and alcohol. It was women in this region who raised the slogan: "Planning without fodder, fuel and water is one-eyed planning". A campaign to fight male alcoholism has also been launched. And in some villages women are demanding an equal say with men in village decision-making, especially on forestry issues, and asking: Why aren't we members of the village councils? (Jain, 1984). The Chipko movement thus has the potential for growing from an ecology movement to one which calls for an end to exploitation at several levels.

At the same time, one cannot ignore the specificities of the Chipko area. The movement essentially involves hill communities which are not characterized by sharp class and caste inequalities, and where women in particular have always played a significant role in the agrarian economy without being subject to the rigid norms of seclusion typically prevalent in the plains of North-West India. It is questionable whether elsewhere in India, in a different socioeconomic context, such community mobilization would be as readily possible.

In this context, it is also noteworthy that the two best-known examples of social forestry in Asia that may be termed successful on a country-wide basis, and not just in localized schemes or areas, are South Korea and China. The two countries differ widely in their political systems, but in both of them the schemes were introduced within relatively egalitarian structures, brought about by radical agrarian reforms undertaken in the 1950s. Of course their ability to implement the reforms or to mobilize the people for community schemes cannot be separated from their political systems or from their cultural backgrounds.

In much of South Asia, however, there is a highly unequal distribution in the ownership and control of land, which usually constitutes the main source of wealth and represents the principal source of economic and political power, especially in the rural areas of these societies. In the absence of redistributive land reform, community involvement in such schemes is likely to be extremely difficult in most cases, and in some perhaps not feasible. This is borne out not only the forestry-related programmes but also by the vast literature on rural development schemes in general which points to the failure of co-operative ventures to benefit the poor, in the Indian subcontinent and elsewhere, unless the co-operatives are composed of people relatively equal in economic and social terms.

With existing village level inequalities there is in fact a danger of promoting farm forestry which typically does not offer a real solution to the fuelwood crisis and can have several undesirable consequences (as discussed below).

Farm forestry

In recent years, the much-quoted success stories of tree-planting projects in India relate to planting on private land for commercial use, such as in Gujarat and Uttar Pradesh (UP). In Gujarat, under the World Bank-aided project mentioned earlier, between 1980–81 and 1982–3, 32,000 hectares were planted under farm forestry, about twice the area targeted, while the achievements in village self-help woodlots fell short of targets by 57 per cent. The bulk of these private plantings have been undertaken by the better-off farmers on land previously under crops and often irrigated. The species planted (eucalyptus is a favourite) are fast-growing and commercially in great demand, as the prices of poles and pulpwood have escalated in recent years. The actual gains have accrued to only 6 per cent of Gujarat's 2.4 million farm families. While tree-planting on government-supervised woodlots has also been reasonably successful, there is no certainty that such wood will be made available to the people, and at a sufficiently low price.

The case of UP is similar. Here, between 1979–80 and 1982–3, the area planted under farm forestry was 3,433 per cent of that targeted, while village self-help woodlots fell short of targets by 92 per cent. the most responsive farmers were those with holdings of 2 hectares of more and the trees planted were again commercial species for providing building poles (World Bank 1983b). Both these have been termed "social forestry" projects but in effect have done little to satisfy the aims of social forestry – namely the provision of fuelwood, etc., for the domestic needs of the rural people.

In fact the schemes can have several dangerous long-term consequences. First, the shift of large areas of fertile land irrigated and rainfed) from food to commercial wood production will reduce the availability of food and fibre in the country. These shifts have been observed in States other then Uttar Pradesh and Gujarat. In the semi-arid Kolar district of Karnataka, for example, Bandyopadhyay (1981) notes that several thousand hectares of agricultural land have been shifted from crops to sericulture and commercial forest plantations. Today, in Kolar district, 16,216 hectares (86 per cent irrigated) is under mulberry, about 20,000 hectares under eucalyptus and 6,710 hectares under casuarina. The most significant shift has been from *ragi*, the staple millet crop of the people, to eucalyptus; farm area under *ragi* in this district is observed to have declined dramatically in recent years. Eucalyptus is also the species that is to be planted on 45.5 per cent of the 110,000 hectares of farmland that will be afforested under a World Bank-aided social forestry project in the State.

Second, the shift from food crops to tree production (which is less labour-intensive) will reduce employment. In the proposed World Bank-aided Karnataka project, eucalyptus monoculture will lead to an estimated loss of 137.5 million person days of employment (Bandhyopadhyay, 1981). Third, the noted shifts are likely to be ecologically destructive where commercial species, which deplete the soil of nutrients and water, replace the present system of mixed or rotation crop farming (e.g. the *ragi*–pulses–oilseeds rotation) that maintains soil stability. Fourth, farm forestry will have a particularly adverse effect on the poor due to lower employment opportunities, faster-rising food prices, and less access to crop waste for fuel. (Eucalyptus leaves cannot be used for fodder and the wood is unsuitable as a cooking fuel since its burning velocity is too high.) In other words, farm forestry is not only unlikely to solve the problem of fuelwood shortages but will probably accentuate the crisis for the poor.

Yet such schemes are being promoted with short-sighted zeal. In fact the Gujarat project is publicized as *the* success story of *social* forestry in India. And the earlier-quoted mid-term appraisal report for this project, despite noting that farm forestry has been essentially commercial forestry in Gujarat, and that village self-help woodlots (which were the main hope for supplying firewood) have failed, heroically concludes: "It seems possible that if the present momentum is maintained, it will be possible to resolve the rural fuelwood crisis in Gujarat within a decade" (World Bank, 1983a).

In many cases such schemes are being defended on grounds of profit maximization. Some note that farmers in Gujarat can annually earn Rs.15,000 per acre or more with eucalyptus relative to Rs.1,000 or less with groundnuts, and conclude that this profit motive must be encouraged still further (Bapat, 1983). Others argue that after a point there will be a glut in eucalyptus, leading farmers to diversify their plantations and grow other species (Jha, 1983: World Bank, 1983a). However, thus far, demand considerably exceeds supply; and in any case, since it is the profit motive that is sustaining eucalyptus production, it is unlikely that slow-growing trees, which will not yield similar short-term gains, will be planted subsequently. Also, yields (whether of other tree crops or agricultural crops) on the land left depleted by monoculture eucalyptus plantations are likely to be low, unless adequate investment is undertaken to restore soil fertility.

The fact is that the current farm forestry policy in India is not the answer to the problem of firewood shortages faced by the poor. At the same time, the issue of social forestry is intricately linked to the social structure and mechanisms of socioeconomic control which determine *who benefits* and *to what extent* from the use of scarce resources. It cannot, as one observer rightly notes, "be reduced to a simple ritual of planting trees" (Agarwal, 1983).

CONCLUDING COMMENTS

It is amply clear that the success of social forestry schemes – the planting of trees to increase available supplies of firewood for the local population – is crucial to alleviating the domestic fuel crisis. At the same time, as with many other rural development programmes, the issue of increased firewood production needs to be linked structurally to that of distribution if the schemes are to fulfil their intended aim. De-linking the two aspects, as has happened in the thrust towards farm forestry in India, has meant not only that the benefits of increasing production go to only a few, but that the product itself is inappropriate for fulfilling domestic fuel needs. Social/community forestry provides the potential for making this link between production and distribution. But the success of such schemes, as noted, requires close community involvement and participation, ideally at all levels and at every stage in scheme implementation.

Such involvement has been circumvented in most cases by (a) the top–down method of scheme implementation characteristic of the implementing bureaucracy, especially the Forestry Department, and (b) the hierarchical socioeconomic structures of the communities in which the schemes are located. We have seen that the causes for project failure lie not in the antagonism between people and trees, but in the antagonism and differential interests between people and people: between the forestry officials and tribal communities, between different class and kinship groups in the village, and so on. Successful projects have emerged precisely where the material basis for such antagonism (especially in terms of land-ownership patterns) has either been eroded, say through a radical agrarian reform programme, or has not existed historically to the same extent (say among more egalitarian hill communities).

In the very recent period in India there has been some move to incorporate the concerns of the poor and landless in forestry schemes, such as the allotment of plots of government-owned degraded forest land or wasteland to small numbers of landless families for planting trees, as in West Bengal and Madhya Pradesh. These families do not have ownership rights to the land but have usufructuary rights to the trees they plant, and seedlings and wages (or a stipend) are given in the initial period. In a few instances, groups of women have also been given wastelands for growing herbs. Mining, too, has been stopped in several areas to prevent further environmental degradation. However, in most cases these steps are the fruits of a concerted struggle by and pressure from local non-government activist groups; and at best, these measures remain concessions, and deviations from the national picture.

Alongside these measures several States are proposing to lease out large tracts of degraded forest land to paper mills for afforestation, to provide pulp, and Karnataka has already taken a lead by leasing out 30,000 hectares to the Mysore Paper Mills (CSE, 1985:73–9). At the *national* level, undeniably, the thrust of forest policy and implementation in India remains orientated to commercial needs. And this thrust is inseparable from the country's overall development strategy, which defines the priorities between sectors, products and technologies used for producing these products (with their associated implications for sources and levels of energy use).

The questions that then arise are: How can this development strategy be altered to take account of environmental concerns in general and the needs of the rural poor in particular? What would be the economic trade-offs of alternative strategies for the country as a whole, and for different classes and social groups within it? What would be the political constraints and feasibilities of alternative paths? These are questions that clearly have no easy answers, but it is imperative to probe them. So far they have not been addressed explicitly by planners or even by most activist groups in South Asia. Hence, on the one hand schemes are ostensibly being instituted to alleviate the firewood crisis facing the poor, on the other hand the existing plan priorities, development policies and their implementation are accentuating the crisis. We encounter once again the familiar paradox.

REFERENCES

Agarwal, Anil, "In the Forests of Forgetfulness", *The Illustrated Weekly of India* (Bombay, November 13–19, 1983.

Agarwal, Anil and Priya Deshingkar, "Headloaders: Hunger for Firewood – I", *CSE Report* No. 118, Centre for Science and Environment (Delhi, 1983).

Agarwal, Bina, *Cold Hearth and Barren Slopes: The Woodfuel Crisis in the Third World* (London, Zed Books, and Allied Publishers, India, 1986a).

Agarwal, Bina, "Women, Property and Agricultural Growth in India", *Journal of Peasant Studies*, vol. 13, no. 4, 1986.

Bahuguna, S., "Women's non-violent power in the Chipko Movement", in Madhu Kishwar and Ruth Vanita (eds.), *In Search of Answers: Indian*

Women's Voices from Manushi (London: Zed Books, 1984).

Bajracharya, Deepak, "Deforestation and the Food Fuel Content: Historico-Political Perspectives from Nepal", *Working Paper*, Resource Systems Institute, Honolulu: East–West Centre, 1983).

Bandhyopadhyay, Jayanto, "Beyond the Firewood March", in *Financial Express*, 1–2 September, 1981.

Bapat, Shailaja, "It Lacks Vitality", *The Economic Times*, India, 6 August, 1983.

Bhaduri, T. and V. Surin, "Community Forestry and Women Headloaders", in *Community Forestry and People's Participation – Seminar Report*, Ranchi Consortium for Community Forestry, 20–22 November, 1980.

BRAC, The Net: Power Structure in Ten Villages (Dhaka: Bangladesh Rural Advancement Committee, 1980).

Briscoe, John, "Energy Use and Social Structure in a Bangladeshi Village", *Population and Development Review*, vol. 5 no. 4, December 1979.

Cernea, Michael, "Land Tenure Systems and Social Implications of Forestry Development Programmes", *World Bank Staff Working Paper* no. 452, April 1981.

Chand, Malini and Rekha Bezboruah, "Employment Opportunities for Women in Forestry", *Community Forestry and People's Participation – Seminar Report* Ranchi Consortium for Community Forestry, 20–22 November 1980; Swaminathau . . .

CSE, *The State of India's Environment 1984–85: The Second Citizen's Report*, New Delhi: Centre for Science and Environment, 1985.

Desai, Ashok V., *India's Energy Economy: Facts and their Interpretation. Bombay: Economic Intelligence Services, Centre for Monitoring Indian Economy, February 1989).*

D'Monte, Darryl, "Pine for the Forest", The Hindustan Times, 4 January, 1982.

Dogra, Bharat, *Forests and People* (Janakpuri, New Delhi: Bharat Dogra, A-2/184, 1984).

Eckholm, Erik P., "The other energy crisis", *World Watch Paper* no. 1, (USA: World Watch Institute, 1975).

Guha, Ramachandra, "Forestry in British and Post-British India – A Historical Analysis", *Economic and Political Weekly*, 29 October 1983.

III

WOMEN AND WATER

5

WOMEN, WATER AND SANITATION
United Nations International Research and Training Institute for the Advancement of Women (INSTRAW)

Inadequate water and sanitation facilities constitute some of the most critical problems faced by the developing world today. Statistics illustrate better than anything else just how devastating these problems are. In this decade, approximately 80 per cent of all sickness and diseases can be attributed to inadequate water supply and sanitation (WSS) facilities. Diarrhoeal diseases alone kill between five and six million children in developing countries every year, and up to eighteen million people in general. More than 400 million people have gastroenteritis, while dysenteries and parasitic worms infect nearly one-half of the entire population of developing countries. People suffering from waterborne disease alone occupy half of all the hospital beds worldwide, and 25,000 of them die every day – representing some 15 per cent of all hospital deaths.

In 1980, three out of five persons in developing countries, excluding China, had no access to safe drinking water, and only one out of four had some sort of sanitation facility. In rural areas, which are significantly worse off than cities, some 30 per cent of the population had access to safe water, but only 13 per cent had suitable sanitation facilities.

Women, as the primary water carriers, managers, end-users and family health educators, play a paramount role in WSS management. By virtue of their domestic functions, they are in constant contact with polluted water and are therefore the group most vulnerable to water-related diseases.

In developing countries, women and children often spend eight or more hours a day fetching polluted water from water supplies which, because of drought, become increasingly distant. Women and girls are also responsible for preparing and cooking food, cleaning utensils, washing children, disposing of babies' faeces and scrubbing latrines.

Involving women in the planning, operation and maintenance of wss facilities is therefore crucial. With a safe, reliable and convenient water supply, they will be able to rechannel vast amounts of time, energy and labour into more productive pursuits. With education and the provision of a clean water supply, women will learn that the suffering, disease and death caused by dirty water can be avoided and family health and hygiene improved by using pure water.

The onerous tasks of women in subsistence farming can also be alleviated by the provision of water supply and irrigation. They will be able to grow more diverse crops that offer better nutrition and supplemental income from the sale of excess food. Similarly, a reliable water supply will enable reforestation programmes to be implemented, which will eventually allow women to use the time and energy previously invested in gathering firewood to replant trees. And if water can be used by men to increase their traditional cash-crop farming, there may be less need for them to migrate to urban areas in search of employment. Fewer women would have to struggle as the sole supports of their households, nor would they have to accept low-paid work on neighbouring commercial farms.

With the availability of water, too, livestock raising and dairy production are possible. Animals can then be used in the fields to reduce women's labour and improve family nutrition.

wss development, in other words, is multidimensional. Its ramifications extend beyond matters of health and environment into the socioeconomic, technical and scientific spheres. All these areas are interconnected: a problem that exists in one will often influence circumstance in the others.

The continued success of any water-supply project involves community participation. Since women are the primary movers of water, they need to be trained in the basic maintenance of facilities and their surroundings. The main issue is not incorporating women into these activities: they are already active participants. Rather, women's participation must be made more effective, easier and more productive. These are the basic premises underlying INSTRAW's work in WSS projects and programmes, and also come into play in the activities of the UN Water Decade, discussed elsewhere in this chapter.

PRESENT PROBLEMS

Despite their important and multiple roles, women are currently not adequately involved in Decade activities. Present problems that must be dealt with include the following:

Not enough attention has been given to women as the primary human resource and the ultimate users of water. Their water-related work is taken for granted and denied an economic and social value. Most women do not have enough water for daily needs; even where it is in short supply, it might be polluted and cause ill health – both for women and for their entire families and communities.

Women are often excluded from the planning and implementation of WSS projects; such projects may lack elements of communication and information on women and the relation between water, sanitation and health practices needed if WSS facilities are to improve general health.

WSS technologies often do not consider the cultural context and level of know-how of the communities, nor are they cognizant of women's needs, interests and skills. Lack of consultation with women regarding technical aspects results in impractical solutions and the overall failure of expensive WSS facilities: pump handles, for instance, may be too heavy or placed too high for women and children to reach them.

Local women's customs, preferences and traditions are not considered in choosing the technical design and location of projects. For example, in some cultures women would not wish to wash themselves in full view of villagers, and yet male engineers often place the pumps in the village square, thinking that was the most convenient location.

121

WOMEN'S ROLES IN WSS PROJECTS

What are the traditional roles women play in community water projects, and how can they be enhanced, to benefit themselves and their communities?

- **Assessing needs.** Although it might seem like common sense to assess the local people's needs before planning and implementing a project, this is not always done. In one project in Guinea-Bissau, planners took the trouble to do this, with great success. Villagers were trained as promoters to encourage others to use the safer water supply. Because the planners knew that promoters had to be respected in their communities, they chose women with children, or older women, instead of young women. In villages where promoters contacted women individually, more people used the new wells. The wells were also conveniently located, since the people had influenced their location. And the fact that some villages were more concerned with irrigation for their rice fields or vegetable gardens than with drinking water was taken into account. As a result, vegetable gardening has flourished to the extent that seeds are sold in the village, improving women's income.

- **Identification of water sources.** Women should be consulted when investigations for development of water resources are undertaken in a community. Their knowledge of water sources and water quantity during dry and wet seasons, and their assessment of smell, taste, colour and convenience, can assist in the final choice of sites. They may be aware of alternative sources; in Panama, for example, village women led engineers to a fresh-water source on the shore of an island which had not been identified in the initial survey.

- **Choice of technology.** For projects to be successfully implemented, women must be consulted regarding their preferred choice of facilities for latrines, washing, watering animals, growing vegetables, etc. In rural Iran, communal laundry facilities built were large rectangular sinks, at adult waist height. However, Iranian women traditionally wash clothes and dishes in a squatting position. As a result, the laundry basins were not used. In Yucatan, Mexico, engineers recommended a squat-plate latrine instead of a pour-flush latrine because they thought women would refuse to carry water from the standpipe to the latrine. However, the women in fact rejected the squat-plate and preferred the pour-flush. Similarly, in Nicaragua, a latrine was not used by women because their feet could be seen from the outside. This could have been avoided if they had been consulted beforehand on the design of the latrines.

- **Operation and maintenance**. Maintenance is an inevitable requirement of any water-supply project which depends on mechanical equipment, and failure of water-supply systems can frequently be attributed to constant breakdowns due to lack of proper operation and maintenance. These breakdowns have resulted in frustrations for women who are forced to walk even longer distances to another source or to revert to the traditional, often polluted sources. In addition, because many women are at home during the day, they are often the best suited to supervise the quality of maintenance work and to protect facilities against vandalism and unintended or mischievous damage by children.

In Angola, for example, where women have been recruited as water-source monitors, the breakdown rate has declined significantly. And in India, a village handpump maintenance project for deep wells was developed. However, the young men trained as caretakers were not the ones to collect water, nor did the women know who the pump caretaker was. The most effective group of caretakers turned out to be a voluntary women's group.

Women have been successful managers of water systems, as the following example from Honduras shows. *Barrio* women headed up a community action committee which got the city authorities to install four standpipes in their hillside slum. They put two standpipes near the top of the hill and two near the bottom, protected by little wooden shacks. One of each pair is open five hours each morning, and the other five hours in the afternoon. Community women, usually from a female-headed household, are hired by the committee on a rotating basis to be in charge of the standpipes, collect set fees for water and keep the water sites clean.

Government policy should, therefore, recognize the important role women can play in operation and maintenance and train them in those areas from the earliest stages of a project on, as they are the first to know when a system is malfunctioning and the most affected by breakdowns. Again, because of their traditional role as providers of water for the family, women caretakers have demonstrated interest, enthusiasm and ability to keep the water system working.

- **Backup support**. In nearly all cultures, women provide backup support to construction workers in the form of food, water and lodging. They motivate and support men to do unskilled voluntary construction work. In Latin America, Africa and parts of Asia, women have willingly volunteered labour in the construction of facilities, especially piped water supplies. In Malawi, women provide up to 70 per cent of the labour in most piped water schemes. In Panama, where a project trained and educated women to participate in the piped water system, the women contributed during construction by carrying heavy loads of sand and preparing food for labourers. They were also involved in maintaining the system and in several communities they collected water fees, and in the process emerged as local leaders.

- **Water conservation**. Water-conservation techniques are crucial where water sources are scarce, which applies to much of the developing world, located in arid and subtropical regions. Because women have high stakes in seeing that there is sufficient water, they can be motivated to support water-conservation techniques that will improve the supply. In Burkina Faso, for example, they helped build earthen dams by collecting the rocks and preparing the gravel and stones needed for construction.

- **Employment of women**. Women can benefit directly from employment possibilities created by a water-supply project. In India, for example, some 200,000 women were registered as labourers in the construction industry, which provides much of the workforce involved in digging wells, installing pumps, etc.

- **Sanitation promotion and education**. The health benefits arising from improved water supplies may not be fully realized unless there are complementary inputs in the field of sanitation, since inadequate sanitation or sewage treatment plays a part in the transmission of many water-related infections. In Pakistan, integrated water and sanitation programmes have been successful, partly because women have been trained as sanitation promoters. Their duty is to motivate and help promote latrine-building in the villages, and while male strangers are not allowed to enter houses and talk to village women, the women promoters are able to enter the houses with ease.

Not surprisingly, women are the most effective promoters and educators in programmes where they are the primary focus, as they generally understand more intuitively the problems and issues faced by other women and can communicate with them more openly. They are also more sensitive to social pressure from other women to do a good job. In one successful village water-supply programme in Mexico, for example, the continued operation and improvement over two decades is due in great part to young women who assisted in the early planning stage, and to local women whom they trained to become active members of the water committee.

Programmes which integrate water supply, sanitation and public health education have multiple benefits. A Bolivian project trained indigenous women to administer immunizations, provide information on child nutrition and lecture on the proper maintenance of wss facilities. One result of this was that a number of these young women were reportedly in complete charge of repair and maintenance of the facilities.

- **Sanitation acceptance and use**. In sanitation, demand for privacy is a determining factor in latrine acceptance by men and women alike, especially in densely settled communities. Women also maintain latrines or supervise maintenance by children, provide hand-washing facilities, take care of excreta disposal and hygiene of young children and assist and educate them in correct latrine use. Factors influencing latrine acceptance and use include the desire to avoid visibility, cost, acceptable arrangements for sharing, status location, appropriateness for children and ease of operation and maintenance.
- **Funding sources**. While financing for wss projects traditionally comes from governments, UN agencies, international development

banks and national lending institutions, women's organizations have begun to take an initiative in providing innovative approaches to funding. In many cases, voluntary groups take on tasks that are officially the government's responsibility. In a Tamil community in India, for example, a nursery-school teacher has been made the pump caretaker, and a women's group pays for the repairs. The voluntary agency that implemented the project has a cadre of women workers trained as pump caretakers based in about forty villages. The agency also employs a mechanic to whom the women report more serious problems.

Where traditional funding is lacking, the women themselves make in-kind contributions of labour and possibly materials, particularly in small, rural areas. Women contribute to savings in construction costs both directly and indirectly. In Kenya, where women do much of the agricultural work of 311 "self-help" projects, 41 per cent of the contributors were women, and they contributed most of the labour – 5,000 hours in two water projects alone.

• **Women's organizations**. National women's organizations can fulfil several functions on a large scale that would not be possible at the community level. They can monitor and campaign for increased government commitment to wss programmes, advertise programme goals and activities in the media, provide assistance in recruiting women managers, engineers and teachers, hold training workshops, raise funds and support local women's groups with funds, equipment, technical backup and information materials.

SUGGESTIONS FOR DEVELOPMENT PLANNERS

Women can participate in the local management and maintenance of wss projects in four major areas: (1) site management: as individual users and as members of user organizations; (2) caretaking: as members of male-female teams with culturally appropriate divisions of tasks; (3) local administrations: as members of local management committees for men and women; (4) self-sufficient systems: operating, managing and maintaining services.

In evaluating the impact of water projects on women, a number of basic questions must be asked. Do women derive economic benefits from the time saved by the projects? How do they use the time for income-generating activities? Do women achieve health improvements, such as more time to care for children; more water for washing and bathing; more knowledge of, and changed behaviour in, water usage, personal hygiene, food preparation, environmental cleanliness and waste disposal? Do they receive any income during the construction of the project, and do they learn new skills?

The involvement of women in wss training programmes must include the following aspects:

(1) Special provisions must be made for recruiting a certain percentage of women as trainees. (2) Special measures are needed to facilitate women's participation in training, such as locating training sites in their villages and providing simple childcare facilities. (3) Women must be trained as trainers at the village level in order to reach other women. (4) Since more women than men work as community volunteers, the community should be mobilized to support them either in cash or in kind or exemption from obligatory labour. If this is not possible, they should be given recognition or appreciation. (5) In training community-level health workers, every effort should be made to promote collaborative activities integrating water and sanitation components in the primary health care and health and hygiene education programmes. Accordingly, institutional responsibility for training must be shared. And in this regard, women must be educated not only as users but also as promoters and educators; existing social structures must also be taken into account.

There are many examples of successful solutions to regional water supply problems that have also had a positive impact on the environment and the socioeconomic well-being of women and their communities. In virtually all of these projects women's participation has been given high priority. When properly trained, women have proven to be successful pump caretakers, latrine-builders, pipe-layers, fund-raisers, educators, and so forth – all occupations that extend far beyond their traditional roles. Clearly, success depends largely on them.

UN Water decade: the task force on women

The United Nations General Assembly at its 1980 session proclaimed the period 1981–1990 as the *International Drinking Water Supply and Sanitation Decade* (IDWSSD), during which Member States were to assume a commitment to improve substantially the standards and levels of services of water supply and sanitation by the year 1990.

The basic principle underlying the IDWSSD is that people cannot achieve a quality of life consistent with human dignity unless they have access to safe drinking water and sanitation facilities, and that such access is a basic human right. In 1982, a *Task Force on Women and the IDWSSD* was set up in recognition of the important role that women play in WSS activities.

Initially, UNICEF and INSTRAW had joint responsibility for the Task Force's secretariat. This role has now been transferred to the UNDP/PROWWESS project *Promotion of the Role of Women in Water and Environmental Sanitation Services*, working in close collaboration with INSTRAW.

Between 1984 and 1986, Task Force member agencies carried out or proposed a number of specific activities to involve women in operational country-level programmes. One proposal called for developing training courses for women volunteers in Sri Lanka, while a project in Bangladesh trained women volunteers from urban slum areas on improved hygiene and health-related practices. A proposed study for India would look at community participation in low-cost sanitation schemes; in Yemen Arab Republic, a hygiene education strategy project is under way for use with rural development projects that include WSS components. A Kenyan organization is training community women in health education and handpump maintenance, and Niger and Senegal are training women in irrigation techniques and repairs. Jamaica offers training courses on water and waste management, while Colombia is preparing female health workers for leadership roles in the formal health sector.

Other areas of activity include workshops, publications of research and case studies, preparation of guidelines and training materials and evaluation of the impact of water projects on women.

Where has the water gone?

Moving rapidly from profligacy to greater efficiency and equity in agriculture's use of water is the surest way to avert shortages and lessen irrigation's ecological toll. Farming accounts for some 70 per cent of global water use. Much of the vast quantity diverted by and for farmers never benefits a crop: worldwide, the efficiency of irrigation systems averages less than 40 per cent.

Each year, some 3,300 cubic kilometres of water – six times the annual flow of the Mississippi – are removed from the earth's rivers, streams, and underground aquifers to water crops. Practised on such a scale, irrigation has had a profound impact on global water bodies and on the cropland receiving it. Waterlogged and salted lands, declining and contaminated aquifers, shrinking lakes and inland seas, and the destruction of aquatic habitats combine to hang on irrigation a high environmental price.

Mounting concern about this ecological toll is making new water projects increasingly unacceptable. And ironically, the degradation of irrigated land through poor water management is forcing some land to be retired completely, offsetting a portion of the gains costly new projects are intended to yield.

By far the most pervasive damage stems from waterlogging and salinization of the soil. Without adequate drainage, seepage from un-lined canals and overwatering of fields raises the underlying ground-water. Eventually, the root zone becomes waterlogged, starving plants of oxygen and inhibiting their growth. In dry climates, evaporation of water near the soil surface leaves behind a layer of salt that also reduces crop yields and, if the build-up becomes excessive, kills the crops.

The degradation of irrigated land from poor water management is forcing some land to be retired completely.

In much of the world, falling water tables signal that ground-water withdrawals exceed the rate of replenishment.

Groundwater levels are falling up to a metre per year in parts of the North China Plain, an important wheat-growing region. Heavy pumping in portions of the southern Indian state of Tamil Nadu reportedly dropped water levels as much as 25–30 metres in a decade; in the western state of Gujarat, overpumping by irrigators in the coastal districts has caused saltwater to invade the aquifer, con-taminating village drinking supplies.

Source: Excerpted from Postel, Sandra, "Saving the Water for Agriculture", *The State of the World, 1990* (Washington DC: Worldwatch Institute, 1990).

Taking matters into her own hands

Bu Eroh, a fifty-year-old woman from a small village in Indonesia, almost single-handedly undertook the manual construction of a conduit to bring water from a spring to her village 4.5 kilometres away.

There was a severe water shortage in her village. Without an adequate water supply, Bu Eroh could plant only cassava and sweet potatoes on her half-hectare dryland plot. She was the family breadwinner for three children and an invalid husband.

In her wanderings to gather mushrooms, Bu Eroh found a spring at a distance of about 20 metres from her home (a two-hour walk). Instinct told her that if a conduit could be constructed, she could divert some of the water to her field. With enough water, she could grow rice.

To divert the water from its source, she had to cut through 45 metres of mountain rock. In doing so, she had to anchor herself on a steep sandstone slope, by tying one end of a rope to a tree at the top of a cliff, and strapping the other end to her waist. If the rope broke, it could mean a 17-metre drop into the rapids of the Cilutung river.

Bu Eroh worked alone for forty-five days, anchored by rope to the slope, chiselling away at the 45-metre-long, 75-cm-wide channel. When people from the village saw what she had done, nineteen men joined in to bring the water through 4 kilometres of rough terrain and over eight hills by building a two-metre-wide canal, under her supervision.

It took two and a half years, but finally the clear spring water arrived. With a dry-season source of irrigation, village rice cultivation expanded from 10 to 15 hectares. Seventy-five hectares in neighbouring villages also benefited. And Bu Eroh expects to reap a ton of rice during her third harvest on the newly irrigated land.

For her work, Bu Eroh received the Kalpataru Award, a national award presented by the country's president to citizens who have "demonstrated extraordinary efforts to maintain and enhance the quality of the environment". The award comes with a 2.5 million rupiah (us$1500) cash prize.

Source: Depthnews Women's Feature, Philippines, cited in "Women and Water", a publication of the International Women's Tribune Centre, July 1990.

Traditional methods of water purification in India

For centuries, nature's various products and women's knowledge of their properties have provided the basis for making water safe for drinking in every home and village of india. In both the oral and written traditions knowledge of these alternative methods of water treatment is still available. The *Susbruta Sambita* lists seven modes of purifying water, among which is the clarification of muddy water by natural coagulants such as the nuts of the *nirmali* tree (clearing-nut tree – *Strychnos potatorium*). The seeds of the *nirmali* tree are used to clear muddy water by rubbing them on the insides of vessels in which it is stored. Seeds of *honge* (*Pongamia glabra*) are similarly used. The drumstick tree (*Moringa oleifera*), which provides a very nutritious vegetable, produces seeds which are also used for water purification. (This tree has travelled from India to Africa as a water purifier, and in Sudan is called the clarifier tree.) *Moringa* seeds inhibit the growth of bacteria and fungi. Since the drumstick is a food, it does not create any risk of toxicity, as chemicals do. Other natural purifiers include *amla* (*Phlanthus emblica*), whose wood is used to clear small rain-ponds in the Indian peninsula. In Kerala, wells are cleared with burnt coconut shells. The *tulsi* (*Ocimun sanctum*) is a water purifier with anti-bacterial and insecticide properties. Copper or brass pots are what Indian women use to bring water from the source, and for storage; unlike plastic, which breeds bacteria, they have antiseptic properties. In Ayurvedic medicine, small doses of specially prepared copper powder are an ingredient of medicines used for diarrhoea, cholera and typhoid. The technologies women have used for water purification are based on locally available natural products and locally and commonly available knowledge. The *honge*, *nirmali* and drumstick trees are partners with women in the safe and easy cure of everyday illnesses like diarrhoea, which can otherwise be fatal.

Natural water purifers and their use in the treatment of water-related diseases

Species	Symptom	Preparation
Acacia catechu	Diarrhoea	Catechu (resinous extract from the wood)
Moringa oleifera	Gastro-intestinal disorders	tea of pounded seeds
	Diarrhoea	pounded seeds in curdled milk
Pongamia glabra	Intestinal worms; parasitic skin diseases	seeds
Strychnos potatorium	Chronic diarrhoea	Half to one seed rubbed into fine paste with buttermilk (internally)
	Eye infections, boils	powdered seed in honey

IV

TAKING ACTION
FOR A BETTER FUTURE

6

THE URBAN CONTEXT: WOMEN, SETTLEMENTS AND THE ENVIRONMENT

Caroline Moser, Frances Dennis and Dulce Castleton

INTRODUCTION
CAROLINE MOSER

I would like to start by saying that I am very honoured to be here and I know I am going to learn a lot. In a sense I feel a bit of an impostor; first because when most of you think of environment, you probably think of rural areas and natural resources. Therefore to talk about the urban or human settlements is something unexpected. Secondly, when we think about the urban environment we think of industrial pollution, air pollution, Bhopal, and not necessarily of human settlements. An additional problem is that the people who work on human settlements to a very large extent have not seen it as an environmental issue, they have seen it as a development issue. I have spent a long time working in human settlements and on issues relating to them – but only now an I rethinking the same problems from an environmentalist point of view. I feel very much at the beginning of this voyage and have been greatly influenced by the thinking of people like Shiva Vandana, Irene Dankelman and Joan Davidson. So what I am going to say to you reflects, in a sense, some thoughts that I have had in trying to relate what I know about urban human settlements to the much more substantive work on environment that has focused on natural resources.

I have been asked to introduce two case studies about human settlements. What we are talking about here is what is called the built, or *man*-made, environment as against the *natural* environment. I will refer particularly to the role of women in mobilizing communities to tackle environmental issues.

From an urban focus I have found it necessary to clarify some fundamental issues about why "women and environment"? In the urban context, the special relationship which women have with the natural environment by virtue of the daily tasks they perform, as Shiva Vandana has written,[1] is perhaps not so obvious. The interlinkages between what she calls the perceived unproductiveness of nature and of women and consequently the devaluation of both is again something that you cannot see so concretely in an urban context. Again, I have had to think very hard about the extent to which women rely on natural systems – soil, water and forestry – for survival and therefore have vested interests in environmental protection and repair, in the urban context.

First of all it is useful to distinguish between women as managers of the traditional environment in other words the areas where they are working to maintain the environment as it already exists; secondly, women as rehabilitators of the natural environment – repairing and taking preventive action to underpin sustainable development, which is both an urban and a rural phenomenon; and finally, as innovators in the use of new, more appropriate, technology in the creation of new environments. Possibly it is this third area that may be most important in the urban context.

Because the special relationship that people have written about is again less visible, possibly planners and policy-makers in the urban context may be more convinced by a focus on gender and development in which the critical starting point is really the different roles that men and women are playing within the environment. Recognition of the fact that men and women often play different roles in society means that we begin to start thinking about the different needs they have and therefore the importance of disaggregating environmental issues on the basis of gender. For instance, taking women's reproductive role and responsibility for childbearing and childrearing: in the urban economy the provision of sustenance to use Vandana's term will require us to look at some sightly different issues, because we are identifying where there is a scarcity of resources. I think the most critical issue in the urban context is land, and access to land. We know that land in the urban context is the prerequisite for access to shelter, probably in a slightly different way from in the rural areas. Where, by tradition or law or whatever, women do not have access to land, this can be a critical determinant of their ability to provide shelter for their family.

We know that the problems of living in environmentally hazardous land conditions in urban contexts are probably the most visible form of environmental issues we see – the gullies, the ravines, the rubbish dumps and the flooded land. The issue of land is a starting point and, as I said, linked to this is the issue of housing. The Third World housing crisis has affected women considerably. The shift in policy-makers' interventions from conventional housing, bulldozing squatter settlements through to sites-and-services, through to upgrading, have had an impact on the sorts of housing to which women have access. We know that there are issues around the design of housing and settlement layout – all of these are concerns that affect women in their reproductive role.

If we turn to their productive role, of course one of the important issues is the zoning of land and the fact that in many urban contexts, where women are working in their houses they are doing so illegally. This is because settlement zoning legislation separates places of work from those of residence.

Finally, if we look at women in their community managing role, we see women as protectors and carers of the community environment. Here, what we are concerned about is the collaborative resource that women have in working together, to challenge authorities, to mobilize, to get access to infrastructure and to basic services. Often it's not so much a matter of them going out and finding resources for themselves, but of them challenging government and the authorities to get those resources.

The two case studies come from Ecuador and Costa Rica and provide comparative as well as contrasting experiences of women's mobilizing role in human settlements. I am going to identify just two or three critical issues. One case study is about the Guarari housing project in Costa Rica; it describes the way in which women's participation in the design as well as the implementation of a new settlement of 3,000 self-build houses ensured that it took account of the environment. In contrast, the Guayaquil (Ecuador) case study is about mobilization by women themselves and the way they have struggled to improve the environment once they have squatted on the land, in this case mangrove swamps. So we have two different issues – one is about what you do to create a new environment, the other what you do to try to improve the environment.

The Guarari study highlights the critical importance of women's reproductive roles in making decisions about house design, the use of community space, the preservation of the natural environment and the improvement of the quality of life. Houses are laid out not in the familiar long lines, but in small groups enabling the women to adapt the natural topography and preserve the habitat.

The Guayaquil case study highlights the importance of women in their community managing role: in the formation, organization and success of local-level protests, challenging the government to provide the necessary infrastructure to improve the environment for their families. Lack of water, electricity, sewerage and, above all roads not only increases the burden of domestic work, but also results in a dangerous and unhealthy environment for their children. Over the past ten years in Guayaquil, women have challenged the local government and the political parties to provide such services.

Finally, in an interesting contrast, the Guarari project shows the important top–down collaborative role of external NGOs (non-governmental organizations), specifically CEFEMINA (a Costa Rican women's group) in building a sense of community and self-help participation with local women, as well as group responsibility for house construction and the management of shared facilities. The evidence suggests that once the social and organizational structure is started, it should be sustainable. How long it is sustainable will be very interesting to see. The community have been living in their houses for a year now.

The Guayaquil experience is a very different one. It is the bottom–up mobilization of community women, with a historical knowledge of organization, in a situation of common suffering.

138

Their mobilization is much more specifically directed at the acquisition of particular items of infrastructure; the organization has gone through dormant as well as active periods. But the fact that they are still active after ten years indicates the enormous sustainability of organizations that women themselves start and use to negotiate for different types of infrastructure.

Both case studies show how important it is that policy-makers should understand why women should be incorporated into environmental policy programmes and projects. How they are incorporated will depend on the manner in which the relationship between women and the environment is recognized. It seems to me that there are a number of distinctions that can be highlighted, and three may be useful for us.

First, if we look at it in terms of welfare:[2] are we concerned with women as victims of environmental degradation who, as passive recipients of assistance, must be helped to ensure that in their reproductive role they can provide a better environment for family welfare? Vandana has, of course, contradicted that whole approach, but in fact if we look at the way women are treated in environmental issues, it may be that there is still quite a tendency to see them as victims of environmental degradation.

Secondly, in terms of efficiency, are women identified entirely in terms of their delivery capacity as the most efficient and effective managers of the environment in both their reproductive and community managing roles? Any measures to enhance their capacity to manage the environment must be careful not to rely on their voluntary time without taking into account their current workloads. Otherwise, the result may be that women are not able to find the necessary time to guarantee success, or at best are forced to extend their working day. My own experience looking at the impact of adjustment in Guayaquil has shown very clearly that women are now having to work more hours in their community managing role, for example in negotiating with NGOs about the delivery of development projects. This is limiting the time they have for reproductive activities, and they still have to earn an income. I think we have to be very careful not to see women simply as efficient at delivering, and therefore collude with the argument that if you want the project to work you work with women.

Finally, the third distinction is about empowering women: recognizing that women are defenders or liberators of the environment, who through greater self-reliance can empower themselves. Measures to assist women to have greater economic and political status to protect the environment are critical if we are to ensure that women are not simply involved in making decisions in communities, but also have equal opportunity to hold office.

My last point is that I think Vandana's comment about the need for restraint rather than rushing in is absolutely critical and I really endorse it. We have seen the "rushing in" to women's income-generating projects, the "rushing in" when there's a new issue. Precisely because of the longitudinal work we have to do in relation to women in the environment, the space to think through the relation between women and the environment is a real warning for us not just to take up the issue and "rush in" again.

NOTES

1. Shiva, V., *Staying Alive – Women, Ecology and Development* (London: Zed Books; New Delhi: Kali for Women, 1988).
2. For a more detailed examination of different policy approaches to women in development see Moser, C., "Gender Planning in the Third World: Meeting Practical and Strategic Gender Needs", *World Development*, vol. 17, no. 11 (1989).

WOMEN'S MOBILIZATION IN HUMAN SETTLEMENTS: CASE STUDY

BARRIO INDIO GUAYAS, GUAYAQUIL, ECUADOR
CAROLINE MOSER

Introduction
In Latin American cities low-income women work not only in their homes and in the factories but also in their neighbourhood communities. Along with men and children they are involved in residential-level mobilization and struggle over issues of collective consumption. The inadequate state provision of housing and local

services over the past decades has increasingly resulted in open confrontation as ordinary people organize themselves to acquire land through invasion, or put direct pressure on the state to allocate resources for the basic infrastructure required for survival. This case study describes the critical role that women play in the formation, organization and success of local-level protest groups.

Acceptance of the sexual division of labour, and the home as their sphere of dominance, has meant that in many parts of Latin America women take primary responsibility for the provision of consumption needs within the family. This includes not only individual consumption needs within the household but also needs of a more collective nature at community level, with the point of residence thus extending spatially to include the surrounding neighbourhood. The extent to which it is seen as "natural" that women should assume such importance in residential-level struggle should be reflected both in the nature of their mobilization and the manner in which it is interpreted. If women's mobilization is perceived as an extension of their realm of interest and power in the domestic arena, then it is most likely that it is in their roles as wives and mothers, rather than as people, that it is legitimized both by the women themselves and by their men.

The development of Guayaquil and the crisis of collective consumption

Within the Ecuadorian economy Guayaquil is the country's largest city, chief port and major centre of trade and industry. It is situated on low land 160 kilometres upstream from the Pacific Ocean. Historically, growth has been linked to the different phases of Ecuador's primary-export-orientated economy. As an industrial enclave, its population growth has reflected the agricultural sector's declining capacity to retain its population as much as the city's potential to create industrial employment. It expanded rapidly during the 1970s at the time of the oil boom because of very high in-migration rates, mainly from the surrounding rural areas. This helped to swell the population from 500,000 in 1960 to 1.2 million in 1982 and an estimated two million in 1988.

Guayaquil's commercial activity is focused around the forty gridiron blocks of the original Spanish colonial city, which in the 1970s were encircled by the inner-city *turgurios* (rental tenements). To the north, separated on higher hilly ground, are the predominantly middle- and upper-income areas, while to the west and south are the tidal swamplands which provide the predominant area for low-income expansion. Settlement of this peripheral zone, known as the *suburbios* (suburbs), involved both the creation of solid land and the construction of incrementally built bamboo and timber houses linked by a complex system of catwalks. With most of the low-income population excluded, in effect, from the conventional housing market (public and private), "invasion" of the municipal-owned *suburbios* was, between 1940 and 1980, the predominant means by which access to both land and a form of shelter was obtained.

Indio Guayas is the name given by the local residents to an area of swampland, about ten blocks in size, located on the far edge of Cisne Dos. The settlement has no clear physical limits, but in 1978 it had some 3,000 residents, the majority of whom belonged to the Indio Guayas neighbourhood or *barrio* committee. In 1978 Indio Guayas was a "pioneer settlement" of young upwardly mobile families, who had moved from inner-city rental accommodation. The community was representative of the lower-paid end of unskilled, non-unionized labour. The men were employed as mechanics, construction workers, tailoring outworkers, unskilled factory workers or labourers, while the women were employed as domestic servants, washerwomen, cooks, sellers and dressmakers.

The motivation to "invade" this municipal floodland and acquire a 10 by 30 metre plot was primarily to own a home and thereby avoid prohibitive rents. The decision to acquire a plot was predominantly a family one. Both individuals and groups were involved in the initial process of cutting back the mangrove swamp and marking out the area. This work was carried out by men, as it was physically arduous and at times dangerous. It was only when the family occupied their plot that women became involved in the process of consolidating their home.

The majority of inhabitants (84 per cent) bought plots on which no house had been built. Consequently, this was a community heavily involved in house construction. A wide knowledge existed not only among professional construction workers but also among most family members. Women made daily repairs to their houses while living in them and children covered holes in the roof and papered the walls with newspaper to keep out the wind. The most important building materials were standardized with corrugated iron roofs, split-cane walls, and wooden floors. Further upgrading was costly and therefore undertaken by few. It involved filling in the swamp under the house, replacing the wood floor with cement, and substituting bricks or breeze blocks for bamboo walls. Families worked on their own homes, with paid labour usually employed in the first, skilled stage of sinking and joining together the mangrove foundations on which the house rests. Although about a quarter of houses in the survey were built by paid labour, over 50 per cent were built mainly by the household, since the skills required were fairly rudimentary.

For most households construction of such a house was accomplished without major difficulties, other than sufficient cash for buying building materials. Far more problematical was the lack of basic infrastructure. it was this that caused communities to protest to the local municipality.

The origins of popular participation
Community-level mobilization in the *suburbios* was neither automatic nor immediate. The development of self-help organization which occurred as areas of swampland were incrementally occupied by a heterogeneous population was the consequence of two interdependent experiences: the common experience within the community of struggling to survive in highly adverse conditions, and varying previous experience concerning the "institutionalized" procedure of petitioning political parties for services in return for votes.

Internal factors. Plots were not always occupied immediately when acquired but were held as a future investment to be occupied when infrastructure had reached the area. The distance from the city centre, lack of electricity, running water, sewerage and above all roads, deterred families from living on their plots. Women were most reluctant to move because of the dangers to children of the perilous system of catwalks, the considerable additional burden of domestic labour under such primitive conditions and the very real fear of loneliness. It was the men, generally less concerned with issues such as these, who persuaded the family to move. But it was the women who bore the brunt, and the distress experienced by many in the early months and years should not be underestimated. Initially, walking on catwalks was so frightening that many crawled on hands and feet, venturing out as infrequently as possible. Acquiring water from the tanker or food from shops up to a mile away were costly, time-consuming and physically gruelling, with women recounting hazardous stories of wading miles through mud to acquire necessary provisions.

It was the struggle for survival in a situation where even water was a scarce and valuable commodity which forced women to develop and retain friendships with their neighbours, and gradually resulted in an increasing awareness among women of the need to try and improve the situation. Although women became aware of their common suffering, this experience itself did not always provide sufficient motivation for common action. Women did not question the fact that their responsibility for the domestic arena, which they saw as natural, made them the primary sufferers.

External factors. The existence of a widely known procedure of petitioning for services in return for votes by self-help committees proved an important external catalyst for instigating popular participation among newly settled communities. The long history of *barrio*-level committees in Guayaquil, beginning in the 1940s, was associated with a political system in which populist parties bought votes by providing infrastructure. Until the late 1960s, committees were short-lived, formed before elections and disbanded soon afterwards. It was only in the late 1960s, with the post-Guevara tremors which shook liberal Latin America, that they took on a more "institutionalized" form. Along with the church, student, and middle-class women's organizations, which flooded the *suburbios* with dispensaries and clinics, came President Kennedy's Alliance for Progress programme. as a condition of a large United States Agency for International Development (USAID) grant for squatter upgrading, the Guayaquil Municipality was forced to create a Department of Community Development whose purpose was to assist poor communities to "fight for infrastructure". The 1972 Plan 240 to infill the mangrove swamps was organized around local *barrio* committees who formed by the hundred to ensure the arrival of infill. Although by 1976, when the project ceased for lack of funds, most committees had disbanded or existed only in name, nevertheless the experience of local organization gained during this period was an important one for the *suburbio* inhabitants.

The role of women in the formation of *barrio* committees

Barrio-level committees in the *suburbios* of Guayaquil contained both women and men members. The *barrio* committee performed a number of functions, particularly in the early stages of settlement consolidation, and it was the women members who took responsibility for much of the day-to-day work. The most important "external" function of the *barrio* committee was to petition for infrastructure, and when the infrastructure was provided, the committee had to ensure that the community's plan of work was implemented. In the committees the women were responsible for this work.

Although it was the women who urged their neighbours to form a committee, they did not automatically see themselves as leaders. Initially, women participated in protest out of desperation at their appalling living conditions. Then, out of a sense of duty, they moved into leadership positions over frustration at the corrupt management of the incumbent men presidents. Women had always formed the overwhelming majority of rank-and-file members. The committee saw itself as a group of predominantly women neighbours working together out of a common preoccupation with their living conditions. Over time, distinctions emerged between those few prepared to take on the difficult responsibility of presidentship and the majority who, for a variety of reasons, preferred to remain working at the rank-and-file level.

Since infrastructure was exchanged for votes, the number and commitment of ordinary members was critical to the success and long-term survival of the *barrio* committee. Although in most families both the men and women joined as members of the committee, it was the women who regularly participated. Where men did attend, their participation was neither regular nor reliable and was often undertaken after considerable pressure had been applied by both the committee and the women.

Political party leaders, administrative officials, and *barrio* men all saw it as natural that most of the participatory work should be undertaken by women: "because women have free time, while men are out at work". Although this may have been true for some, particularly during the daytime, it was also a convenient myth. Most women, throughout their adult lives, are involved not only in domestic and childrearing work but also in a diversity of income-earning activities, even though these are more likely to be undertaken from home. Time spent in mobilization was therefore detrimental both to domestic and to productive work, and women made considerable sacrifices, often risking their jobs as well as neglecting children, in order to participate. This attitude was reinforced by the women themselves. Just as it was natural for them to take full responsibility for domestic work in the home, women saw it as their responsibility to improve the living conditions of their family through participation in *barrio*-level mobilization. Equally they perceived themselves as benefiting most from, for instance, piped water, since the work of water collection and haulage was undertaken primarily by them.

Progress

Although the women of Indio Guayas perceived collective consumption needs in terms of infill, water, electricity, health care and education, these were not prioritized in any particular order. There was a strong sense of political pragmatism, of petitioning for the particular infrastructure they believed they would be most likely to get at any given time in exchange for votes. Since the late 1970s, when the study was undertaken, the *Barrio* Committee achieved the following basic infrastructure:

- The area around and between the blocks has been infilled, although the internal area within each block has not;
- Filling the swamp under the houses has been carried out by most families, individually;
- Access roads surround the neighbouring and have replaced the catwalks;
- Electricity has been installed;
- A piped water system gets to the front of each house, although water pressure is too low to reach indoors.

To date there is still no sewerage system (households have individual septic tanks), drainage system or garbage collection.

Conclusion

Because of the escalating costs of housing programmes, site-and-service projects are not reaching low-income groups, and upgrading or other forms of self help have become more important. These rely substantially on community participation and, as the case study has shown, on the participation of women. It also shows that women participate with clearly defined objectives relating to practical gender needs such as better housing or infrastructure services – needs which are required by all the family but which women in their reproductive, productive, and community-managing roles see as their responsibility to provide.

Extracts from: Moser, Caroline (1987), "Mobilization is Women's Work: Struggles for Infrastructure in Guayaquil, Ecuador", in C. Moser and L. Peake (eds), *Women Human Settlements and Housing* (London: Tavistock Publications, pp. 166–94, 196; Moser, Caroline (1988), "The Impact of Recession and Structural Adjustment Policies at the Micro-Level: Low Income Women and Their Households in Guayaquil, Ecuador", paper originally prepared for UNICEF, New York, pp. 6–7; Moser, Caroline, "Residential Level Struggle and Consciousness: The Experiences of Poor Women in Guayaquil, Ecuador," DPU Gender and Planning Working Paper No. 1, 1985 (London: DPU, UCL, pp. 1–23; Moser, Caroline, "Surviving in the *suburbios*", *Bulletin*, 1981, vol. 12, no. 3 (Sussex: Institute of Development Studies).

WOMEN'S MOBILIZATION IN HUMAN SETTLEMENTS: CASE STUDY

THE GUARARI HOUSING PROJECT, COSTA RICA
FRANCES DENNIS AND DULCE CASTLETON

Introduction

The Guarari Community Development Project is a unique experiment in low-cost housing in the crowded central valley of Costa Rica. It is situated between the capital city of San José and the provincial capital of Heredia. Two non-governmental organizations CEFEMINA, a prominent women's organization, and COPAN, which campaigns for and helps build community housing have stimulated and supported a grass-roots movement which addresses population and natural resources within a wide range of integrated activities. The project illustrates the roles of women, as planners and resource managers.

Ecological significance

The Guarari Community Development Project is located in the fertile central plain of Costa Rica which, until recently, supported most of the agricultural production for the entire country. The government so far has no land-use plan for this region, nor is there an overall strategy to manage increasing urbanization in accordance with the principles of conservation of natural resources. Guarari offers a model for housing low-income families in ways compatible with raising the standard of living of local people, encouraging the acceptance of smaller families and protecting and restoring the natural environment. Pioneered by women, this type of community development offers possibilities for periurban expansion which nevertheless provides a "lung" or "green belt" around large cities, reducing atmospheric pollution. Rural agricultural skills can be preserved and productivity of the land renewed. Interviews with residents and prospective residents of both sexes and all ages suggest the following conclusions about the project:

- It contributes techniques and experience to IUCN's 'toolbox' methodologies, offering a model for managing urbanization in ways harmonious with the principles of conservation;
- It is productive, rather than destructive of the local environment, preserving and increasing the natural vegetation and habitat;
- It creates a conservation mentality in an integrated community, generating a sense of pride in keeping the community "green, clean and beautiful" and laying foundations for the environmental education of young people;

- It encourages smaller families through health education and family planning;
- It strengthens indigenous non-governmental organizations and encourages their participation in conservation activities. Special efforts are being made to save, as much as possible, the natural flora. Each development area of the six into which the site is divided is named after a local tree. The community's symbol is a large shade tree at the entrance. Each house is required to have a garden and there is tremendous pride in the general beauty of the *finca* (the site was originally a coffee plantation). The children are involved in the protection of the existing flora and fauna and in campaigns to plant new trees. For Mothers' Day in 1988, a group of schoolchildren planted trees around the school yard in honour of their mothers.

There is a project to grow and propagate medicinal plants, now in an embryonic stage but with a development plan prepared by the agricultural adviser to the project. A local resident planted the first seedlings and most of the houses now have two or more plants growing. The plan is to establish a large production unit in the watershed area which will not only provide income to resident women but create local knowledge of the use of plants. This can be passed on to the next generation and lead to greater understanding of the uses and limitations of expensive commercial pharmaceutical products.

The management of waste is an important part of the environmental protection programme. Participants are committed to keeping the site free of litter and garbage and have raised funds, through raffles and the sale of old clothes, to buy containers for the waste. An agreement was made with the official services to collect the contents of these waste-disposal units. The use of water- and electricity-saving devices has been proposed by the city planners for future units and incentives will be given to demonstration houses. Results can be measured by comparing the overall natural habitat in Guarari with the other sites where conventional urbanization took place. Guarari is litter-free, with pleasant flower gardens around the houses and well-kept shade and fruit trees. While it is difficult to measure the extent of environmental protection awareness-building among the residents, many people gave evidence that they are quite aware of their responsibilities and of the need to defend their natural resources.

The most ambitious and probably the most significant environmental protection effort, in addition to the promotion of a generally healthy community environment, is the plan to conserve and rehabilitate the watershed area. The community is eager to start on these activities, which include recreational facilities, nature walks and lectures. The watershed management plan has been completed and is to be put into operation as soon as funds are available. Students from the university in Heredia are involved, and a local committee has been organized.

Demographic significance

The population of Costa Rica in 1988 was 2.8 million, having increased by 300,000 in only four years. Most of the people (1.6 million in 1987) are concentrated in the central plain. Density in the western part of the plain, which embraces San José, Heredia and several other cities, is 825 per square kilometre. The population is growing at the rate of 2.9 per cent a year, due to high fertility, low mortality and continuing immigration from the neighbouring countries of Nicaragua and El Salvador. If the rate of growth does not decline, the total population could reach 3.9 million by the year 2000 and 6.7 million by 2025. These figures do not take account of the future trend of immigration. Internal migration continually swells the numbers in the central plain. Some consequences of continuing population growth have been summarized[1] as follows: spread of urbanization on to agricultural land; water shortages; increasing problems of waste disposal; spreading pollution of rivers and streams; increasing problems caused by floods; probable increase in atmospheric pollution.

The government established a National Population Policies Commission in 1968. Family-planning services are provided at hospitals and health centres. Several non-governmental organizations also provide education and services. Some 66 per cent of married women of reproductive age are estimated to practise family planning. However, practice rates are uneven across the country and services for young people are generally lacking. The ambitious and wide-ranging National Conservation Strategy at present being formulated does not address population growth and distribution, although a private-sector initiative is being launched to gather population data in relation to pressures on the national environment.

Guarari is included in the general programme of *Salud Vivencial* (living health) promoted by CEFEMINA in conjunction with other social assistance organizations for the area. This is an integrated approach to health services in which prevention of disease, nutrition, personal and social hygiene and family planning are included. The health committees in the community are responsible for the education and referral services within the group. In Guarari, most of the women and men interviewed were quite familiar with the health activities and vocal about the needs to balance personal interests and needs with scarce available resources. The majority attended the family-planning lectures and several mentioned personal counselling with the physician and other members of CEFEMINA. According to the results of a survey conducted by the *Association Demografica Costarricense* (ADC) in 1988, the areas served by CEFEMINA's living health project, including Guarari, produced higher family-planning acceptance rates than the national average.

Evolution of the project

Successive governments have made attempts, sometimes politically motivated, to cope with the increasing pressure of migrating peasants who had lost their rural lands and were attracted to jobs and the cultural life in the capital city of San José and other main cities, including Heredia, Cartago and Alajuelo. In the 1970s the government established an institute of housing (*Instituto Nacional de Vivienda y Urbanismo* – INVU) which began buying up farms on the periphery of the city for slum-clearance housing.

Installation of urban services and the actions of squatters on these lands were very destructive of the natural environment, since the land was cleared of trees and other natural vegetation. This also created conditions for many social problems. In many cases squatters moved on to the land before the promised housing, water, sanitation and electricity services were installed and without any advance planning for schools, health centres and other social amenities. The government action – or lack of it – therefore gave land indiscriminately to those who were ready to grab it, without consideration for families waiting to move out of the older, squalid living conditions of the original slums.

Neighbourhood groups sprang up to protest at these conditions and this led to the formation of an independent organization to fight for housing (*Comite de Luchapor Vivienda*). This was the forerunner of COPAN, which gathered increasing strength and drew into its ranks not only the disgruntled slum-dwellers but also professionals and students from a wide range of disciplines who sympathized with their plight. Numerous demonstrations were staged in front of the housing institute (INVU) and there were several hunger strikes. They found, and used to advantage, a 1949 amendment to the Rent Act which stated that residents of premises which were incomplete – i.e. without urban services – were exempt from rent payments. COPAN helped residents to take defaulting landlords to court.

In 1981 CEFEMINA was established as an independent, non-political organization dedicated to improving the lives of women. Its fore-runner was the *Movimiento Para Liberacion de la Mujer*, establish-ed in 1974. CEFEMINA's members are women everywhere who want to engage in and benefit from its activities, as well as volunteers from every walk of professional life who are prepared to share their skills, time and experience. CEFEMINA had the advantage of being untarnished by the political battles in which COPAN had had to engage, although its predecessor had been part of the protest movement. CEFEMINA launched its own campaign against the lethar-gic government machinery, opposing the policy of allowing squatter communities, demanding the installation of urban services *before* housing construction took place and asking for virgin land on which to pioneer self-help community development which would preserve the natural environment and improve the quality of human life. CEFEMINA's interest from the start was to build a sense of community self-help, particularly among women, as well as group responsibility for house construction, management of shared facilities and group activities to meet other social needs of the residents.

In 1986 CEFEMINA got its first experimental site at Corina Rodrigues, on the southern fringe of the capital. But here INVU had already proceeded with its conventional plans of small, box-like houses all facing busy access roads. The basic structure and front walls of the houses were already in place, the residents being left to put up the remaining walls, roof and floor. There was no chance to influence the design of the houses, only to mobilize the community to finish the construction work and meet their other social needs through group endeavour. At the next site, nearby Guapil, CEFEMINA was able to persuade INVU to allow an improved plan of construction in order to break the monotony of uniform rows of houses. The modest changes – alternative distances from the road, exposed decorative bricks and variety in roofing styles as well as attractive front gardens – instilled a sense of pride into the community and created a strong feeling of community belonging, involvement and responsibility. This experience, together with other similar activities at Cartago and Alajuela, gave both CEFEMINA and COPAN, its partner in house construction, the experience they needed to become convinced of the importance of trying to meet the total social, housing and environmental needs of the individual and the family.

The campaign for better housing had gone on for eight years. Problems experienced in the earlier project areas were acute – lack of job opportunities, high fertility rates, poor health, social conflicts and antisocial behaviour by young people. The men and women who had emerged as local community leaders were convinced that pre-project planning was essential. The political struggle, protest meetings and hunger strikes had given way to a more purposeful, self-help, action-orientated movement which needed only a relatively modest commitment on the part of the government to allow a pioneering initiative of possibly far-reaching consequences to take place.

CEFEMINA was now working closely with COPAN – the former dedicated to a new concept of community living, the latter convinced by the evidence that a new approach to land use and community hands-on house construction was needed. Women emerged as the main protagonists for community-serving housing arrangements which would stimulate, rather than stifle, group responses to social needs. Thanks to the support and intervention of the Minister of Housing, Dr Fernando Zumbado, the two collaborating organizations were allocated a former coffee plantation near the provincial capital of

Heredia, some 20 kilometres to the north-west of San José. Guarari was born.

Guarari

Guarari comprises 118 hectares of land, nine of which form a watershed area of steep banks of natural vegetation through which a small watercourse traverses the area from east to west. The site has a pleasant exposure towards the surrounding countryside and distant mountains. The land is part of the central plain which previously provided most of the agricultural productivity of Costa Rica.

It is planned to accommodate 3,000 houses which will be part of a new urban metropolitan area. The programme of *auto-construccion* has been developed for impoverished families, many of them headed by women with young children. The houses are planned in *conjunto residencial integrado*, with a variety of designs to break the monotony of uniformity. Each group of houses will have the social and physical facilities necessary for a productive community life. The arrangement of houses into small groups enables them to adapt to the natural topography and preserves the natural habitat as far as possible. Thirty-five houses have already been erected and are now inhabited. A number of temporary houses were put up on the site immediately it was acquired, in order to discourage intruders and provide homes and minimum amenities for a few families who could start sowing the seeds of the new community; these people will eventually be rehoused.

The ravine or watershed (*quenca*) is of special importance. Plans have already been made to preserve and enhance its beauty. Previously a refuse dump, this area is being cleared prior to replanting and a specific subproject for its rehabilitation has been developed for which both ecological and social objectives have been set. The cultivation of medicinal plants and the establishment of a tree seedling nursery are among income-generating activities which will be adjacent to this amenity. Much of the *quenca* is intended as a place of recreation which will be safe and pleasant and discourage the crime and other anti-social behaviour which would otherwise flourish in such an open area. The rehabilitation of the ravine will give the diversity necessary for the total ecological improvement of the area. An important principle of the development of the whole

154

area of Guarari is the preservation of existing trees, many of which are attractive, large-flowered specimens originally planted to shade the coffee.[2]

Auto-construccion – self-help houses

The Guarari project is being developed on the principle that present and future residents build the houses themselves: *auto-construccion*. The government facilitates land acquisition and material; the beneficiaries provide the labour and final finishing of the units. Financial support is provided by the *Banco Hipotecario de la Vivienda* (BANHVI), which is a government credit bank. BANHVI provides the funds for land acquisition by INVU (the Housing Institution) which, in turn, accepted a project proposal from COPAN. COPAN has the capacity to hire technicians, buy materials, work with other organizations involved in social issues and generally administrate the housing developments. CEFEMINA has the philosophical and social structure for group work, especially with women.

A house in Guarari costs 210,000 *colones* (about $2,500). To qualify for a house a head of household needs 900 hours of credits for work done on the site, most of which will be construction work but can also include training in construction work , day-care of children, help in the communal kitchen, road-cleaning and maintenance of services. Having qualified, a beneficiary becomes an affiliate of COPAN and is entitled to draw 155,000 *colones* from BANHVI for the house, 35,000 from INVU for the lot and 20,000 from COPAN for other expenses. A borrower has fifteen years or more to repay the loans for the house and lot. The total cost is subject to a fixed interest rate of no more than 18 per cent per year. A borrower is required to pay no more than 25 per cent of the family's total income; therefore the payments are staggered accordingly and the total time allowed for repayment can be extended. INVU watches the cost of the Guarari experiment carefully. But according to COPAN/CEFEMINA's report, while a house in Guarari costs 210,000 *colones*, one of the same size in Corina Rodrigues costs 310,000. There are important reasons for this difference.

• Houses in Corina Rodrigues were not built in the true sense of *auto-construccion*. A private construction company was hired by INVU to put the streets, water lines, electricity and basic structure of each house into place. For 250,000 *colones*, a family received a unit called *nucleo-humedo*, composed of the base frame, front wall and a connection for a sink and toilet. The family had to finish the house according to its own individual possibilities, adding the other walls, the roof, sink and toilet, at an additional cost of 60,000 *colones* upward, depending upon the ability to find the necessary resources. Many of these houses have never been finished, although CEFEMINA is doing its best to help in this process.

- Each house in Corina Rodrigues has individual status in relation to water and electricity supplies. In Guarari, groups of houses have the status of a condominium, thus reducing the cost of connecting the supplies.

- Land use in Guarari is more efficient: whereas houses in Corina Rodrigues have larger "backyards", the common green areas enjoyed by housing units in Guarari are much larger.

- Labour for house-building in Guarari is contributed by the residents and beneficiaries themselves. They were trained, in the first instance, by a group of hired construction supervisors who live on the project site in temporary housing. In addition to their paid work, they are required to give ten hours of volunteer work per week in order to gain their right to a housing unit. This time is spent passing on construction techniques to others. The number of trained people increased and construction costs fell accordingly.

- In Guarari a warehouse and production unit was established onsite. Standard components such as doors, window-frames and ceilings are produced in this unit, thus reducing the need to buy from private companies.

- Guarari workers have become very cost- and quality-conscious. There is personal interest in optimizing the use of resources, both human and material, and achieving cost-effectiveness.

Measurements of success

The work at Guarari has only just begun. Many more houses have yet to be built. Small-scale industries, such as rabbit-breeding, production of medicinal plants and a nursery for the propagation of tree seedlings, are either at an experimental stage or still to be negotiated. The rehabilitation of the watershed is still on the drawing-board. Water is so far available only for household use. Final success and sustainability cannot yet be measured. Nevertheless, many positive aspects emerged from direct observations and interviews on the project site.

- There is a clear definition of the problem that the project seeks to solve – i.e. the shortage of decent and appropriate housing for low-income families and women heads of household. All participants agree that the goal is to obtain appropriate living quarters in a healthy environment where there are also other facilities to foster a better way of life.

- There is long-term commitment to achieving the goal, most participants having already engaged in the struggle for housing for some seven years. There are signs that in the longer term a change in government attitudes and approaches will come about, as well as official acknowledgement of the need for a futuristic overall social policy and land-management plan.

- Women have taken the lead in overturning the conventional housing designs of government and have negotiated with engineers and financing agencies for units which are better adapted to their needs, allowing proper supervision of children at play, more ventilation in kitchens and other workplaces and communal recreation facilities. They have learnt to question any proposals put forward by government, to assess them against their own needs and to put forward their own counter-proposals with conviction.

- There is strong evidence of close rapport between the participants and the lead organizations, CEFEMINA and COPAN. This is because many participants are members of one or both these organizations and interact with them on a day-to-day basis and at the policy level.

- An effective working structure has evolved. There is a strict system of job allocation and monitoring in the Guarari project. In the beginning, the activities were led by the CEFEMINA/COPAN group; they are now selected by the representatives of the specific committees. Construction activities are very well defined and require little negotiation. However, the mechanisms to accomplish them are dealt with by group discussion. CEFEMINA/COPAN continue to play roles as facilitator and promoter. The two organizations work closely together and meet every week to discuss progress, evaluate plans and decide on actions that are needed. Several members of the executive board come from the target audience. Board members bring the issues to the community leaders, who are mostly women. The women, in turn, bring them to the general assembly for discussion. The assembly meetings are held once a month but can occur more frequently if emergencies arise. All affiliated members are required to participate in one or more committees. The largest is the housing committee, which at this stage of the project has the heaviest agenda. There is also a health committee, an education committee, a recreation committee and a committee on environment issues. Each committee meets once a week and reports back to the general assembly. Committee work counts towards the 900 hours everyone is required to do to qualify for a house, so the work is monitored by assigned group members.

- Increasing numbers of people are being trained in housebuilding – all those interested in heading any of the committees and in the practical skills required for the work. The building group is constantly training members: as construction advances, new skills are needed. In the beginning the training was done by experienced builders, but now a group of trained trainers has been formed to carry this work forward. Construction techniques have been developed on the site as more and more local people have gained technical skills. Many of the men and women interviewed expressed satisfaction with the skills they had acquired through participation in the training programmes. The health/family-planning committee members also showed their enthusiasm for both the methodology and content of the training they received. Both men and women approved of the group approach to health and family planning, since, as one respondent put it, "only in the support groups can one discuss different aspects of family planning and health issues and thus educate each other, which the government can never achieve". Interviewees reported that they had acquired extremely useful skills which they could apply to other unanticipated situations as they arose. The educational achievements, of which training is a continuing part, can be considered one of the most sustainable components of the project. The construction techniques, learnt by men, women and children alike, are a permanent part of local knowledge and thus transmissible to future generations. All those interviewed indicated a willingness to learn and an eagerness to improve their performance. The continuing presence of CEFEMINA and COPAN and their encouragement to local leaders to pursue education and management skills are two of the sustainable elements.

- Incentives are proving effective. The most obvious one is the prospect of home-ownership but the approbation of peer groups, expressed verbally at the general assembly, for such achievements as the neatest house, the best-kept garden and the most community service are highly prized.

- There is a conscious effort on the part of the project's directors to use and generate local resources for the activities. Most of the building material is produced locally and onsite production of doors, window-frames, wall planks and other prefabricated house parts has been successful. All the educational materials have been produced in the office of CEFMINA by volunteer groups. Outside funding is limited mainly to the salary for the doctor and for the materials/equipment used in the family-planning activities. Many of the volunteer activities are carried out by graduate students from the national

159

university who are simultaneously collecting information for their theses. However, the project does raise funds for specific activities; a Spanish feminist group has assisted with the construction of sixteen houses for single young mothers who are heads of households. Everyone, however, helps with the construction of these houses; it is an essential part of the community goals.

- The population is aware of the need to preserve the existing flora and fauna and rehabilitate the watershed area that crosses the site. In interviews, they commented on the lack of knowledge about environmental programmes and the need to develop the basic ingredients of an appropriate school curriculum.

- There is a sense of permanency and continuation. All those interviewed cited the positive learning aspects of the project. Without exception, they affirmed that their lives are better since they have been involved with the project. The experiences gained in community involvement, skills acquired through specific activities and the acquisition of a place to live were the most sustainable aspects of the project. The techniques are the ones familiar to them and are being transferred to others. Ther permanency of the project is reflected in the long-term goals of the activities and the need to conserve and identify new resources. As Guarari is already limited and its houses are allocated, young people interviewed were asked what they will do when they wish to start a family and need a place to live. The answer was that they have learnt how to solve the housing problem for themselves and their own struggle may be easier than that of their parents.

- There is no apparent reason why the experiment at Guarari should not be repeated elsewhere. It would appear to be eminently replicable. Experience at Guarari is showing that this type of community planning is cost-effective and brings many additional benefits to both the inhabitants and the land they occupy. Guarari provides a model for periurban housing around large cities which can help ameliorate atmospheric pollution and provide a "lung" or "green belt" for the city. Government officials expressed themselves satisfied with this model and indicated that, in general, they would be happy to see it followed elsewhere.

Some unresolved issues

The Guarari project began as a struggle and, to some extent, it still is. Participants know that they are under scrutiny to see how they perform and how effectively they manage the resources at their disposal. Government officials, while favourably impressed, still have to be convinced that the Guarari model is the way for the future. There is no firm evidence that the government intends to revise its overall housing policy in this direction. Plans for the development of the watershed hinge on, among other things, a solution to the problem of a permanent water supply, since the watercourse is dry for much of the year. Agricultural production, a tree nursery and the propagation of medicinal plants, as well as the general restoration of the vegetation, will depend on convincing the water authorities to extend supplies beyond the present use restricted to domestic premises. The specialized needs of the environmental rehabilitation plans (including the generation of income-earning opportunities for women) will probably require additional financial support. During 1989 the continuation of family-planning education and services to the area, including the payment of the doctor's salary, was in doubt – due to shortage of funds on the part of the collaborating agency, *Asosiacion Demografica Costariccense* (ACD). Special project funds are being sought to protect this vital sector of the activities. Environmental education materials were non-existent and the project leaders admitted that they lacked the specific knowledge required to develop these. IUCN's help is being sought for guidelines on the development of locally appropriate materials not only to serve the project but also to use it as a testing ground for a broader approach to environmental curricula.

NOTES

1. Data supplied by the Ministry of Mines, Energy Natural Resources programme, including Guarari, produced higher family-planning acceptance rates than the national average. The number of abortions was lower as was the level of child mortality.
2. As already noted, the government has no land-use plan for the heavily populated central plain. The state housing is pushing out on to the most fertile lands, whereas other, less productive land in the direction of Santa Ana, to the West, is underused for this purpose. The Guarari experiment has drawn timely attention to this problem.

Source: This case study is based on information collected in the field by Dulce Castleton and Frances Dennis in March 1989. Twenty-one interviews were conducted with representatives of selected target groups of the project population and lengthy discussions took place with project leaders. The team also met with government officials, representatives of donor agencies and directors of other non-governmental organizations. Maps, blueprints, photographs, video recordings and educational materials were obtained, and these are being held as reference material in the office of the IUCN Population, Women and Natural Resources Programme at Gland, Switzerland, where they are available for consultation.

7

STANDING UP FOR TREES: WOMEN'S ROLE IN THE CHIPKO MOVEMENT
Shobita Jain

The Chipko movement has attracted worldwide attention. The image of poor, rural women in the hills of northern India standing with their arms around trees to prevent them being cut down is a romantic and compelling one. The reality, in many ways, fits the image: the Chipko movement can indeed be considered an important success story in the fight to secure women's rights, in the process of local community development through forestry and in environmental protection. But there are more complicated implications as well. It is important to understand the history of Chipko and the context in which it arose – and is still evolving.

Since no society is found in a state of perfect structural equilibrium, there are always situations of conflict. Each society, moreover, has institutionalized ways and means of articulating and resolving such conflicts. If a need is felt for altering or transforming structures in a certain fashion, some form of collective mobilization of people and their resources is resorted to; such an activity is given the name of "social movement". By contrast, there is also sometimes collective resistance to social change. Social movements, in short, can aim at either changing or preserving the way things are – or both.

In the case of women's role in the Chipko movement, it is both. (*Chipko*, a Hindi word meaning "hugging", is used to describe the movement because local village women literally "hugged" trees, interposing their bodies between the trees and the loggers to prevent their being cut down.) the Chipko movement is an ecological movement, concerned with the preservation of forests and thereby with the maintenance of the traditional ecological balance in the Sub-Himalayan region, where hill people have traditionally enjoyed a positive relationship with their environment. Thus, it strives to maintain the traditional status quo between the people and the environment. Its proponents have tried to demonstrate that the past and present forestry policies of the Indian government have negatively affected the ecological balance of the area and caused the uprooting of indigenous people who previously depended on forest for their survival and preserved the forest by maintaining a strong bond of veneration and love toward it.

The Chipko movement, which has now spread from one end of the Himalayas in Kashmir to the other in Arunachal Pradesh, is endeavouring to alter the government's forestry policy by insisting on maintenance of the traditional status quo in the Himalayan and other forest regions of India. In this sense, there is resistance to change and to an opening up of the area for technological development.

The collective mobilization of women for the cause of preserving forests has brought about a situation of conflict regarding their own status in society. Women have demanded to share in the decision-making process along with men; hence, there has been opposition by men to women's involvement in the Chipko movement. Women are, on the one hand, seeking alterations in their position in society and, on the other, supporting a social movement that is resisting change. To understand this, it is crucial to ask why women support the movement, what the extent of their awareness is, and how many women in the hill areas are actually participating in the movement.

WOMEN AND CHIPKO

Leaders of the Indian independence movement at one stage decided to seek women's participation, and Mahatma Gandhi gave a call to Indian women to come out of their homes to work for the cause. In the Chipko movement, women became involved through a different process. There was a sustained dialogue between the Chipko workers (originally men) and the victims of the environmental disasters in the hill areas of Garhwal (chiefly women). Women, being solely in charge of cultivation, livestock and children, lost all they had because of recurring floods and landslides. The message of the Chipko workers made a direct appeal to them. They were able to perceive the link between their victimization and the denuding of mountain slopes by commercial interests. Thus, sheer survival made women support the movement.

Why men did not see these connections and women did has to do with the way the subsistence economy is organized in this area. It is also related to the way men perceive the Chipko movement as a "back-to-nature" strategy and to their preference for a traditional type of economic development that takes place around them.

However, whether the Chipko workers realized it or not – or intended it or not – the women who participated in the Chipko meetings, processions and other programmes have become aware of their potentialities and are now demanding a share in the decision-making process at the community level.

THE SOCIAL SETTING

The Garhwal division of Uttar Pradesh (one of India's northern States) comprises the four districts of Uttarkashi, Chamoli, Tehri and Pauri and covers a total area of 27,002 square kilometres, with a population of more than 700,000, less than 1 per cent of the total population of the State. Uttarkashi and Chamoli, both border districts with the Indo–Tibetan boundary to the north, are the least-populated districts of the State.

The Indian Social Institute of New Delhi financed a two-month study visit to the Chamoli district by a group including the author in September–October 1982. Chamoli was selected as our unit of investigation because the Chipko movement, initiated by a group of Sarvodaya workers (followers of Mahatma Gandhi's disciple Vinoba Bhave), originated here. The total area of the Chamoli district is 9,125 square kilometres. Ninety-six per cent of the district population lives in villages. There are 1,649 villages in all, and of these 1,488 are inhabited. Of the total population, 58 per cent are gainfully employed. Sixty per cent of the total female population of the district are "working" while only 55 per cent of the men in the district work. Further, 97 per cent of working women are engaged in cultivation, as compared with only 72 per cent of the men.

Not only do females in the Chamoli district outnumber males by four percentage points, but single-member female households outnumber single-member male households. The majority in these single-member households belong to the fifty-plus age group. Male migration from the hill areas to find work in the armed services and other jobs in the plains is fairly common, with women left to look after land, livestock and families.

Subsistence

A visit to the area makes one realize that topographic and climatic conditions require special adaptation by people who have to work extra hard to survive. During the 1982 field trip, seven villages were visited and open-ended interviews held with rural women and men. Unlike that of the villages in the Indo-Gangetic plains, the rural population of this area depends on land as well as forest for its subsistence and other survival requirements. Such dependence makes the character of social life in this region significantly different from that of the rural population in the plains. Nearly every family in the village owns land, usually less than half a hectare. Annual crops grown here are wheat, paddy, pulses and oilseeds. Farming is mainly dependent on monsoon rains rather than irrigation channels.

In general, subsistence farming by an average family of five members is possible for three to six months per year. For the rest of the year, villagers have to look for other sources of subsistence. The nearest source is the forest around them. Thus, settled agriculture is coupled with the foraging of minor forest produce. The villagers also use wood from the forest for various purposes, such as agricultural tools, dwellings, cooking fuel and fodder for grazing cattle. The use of forest products is expected to increase.

People generally had free access to the forest until 1821, when a process of gradual control over the forest area by the government began. Among some nomadic tribal groups, control over territories holding strategic food resources was specified in terms of customary laws, but government policy specified their dissociation "from the management and exploitation of the forest wealth" (Joshi, 1981).

In terms of day-to-day life, the basis for sex-role differentiation and the types of relationship between the sexes are linked with the pattern of cultivation and exploitation of forest wealth. Women's position in the society is governed by the norms of a patriarchal system of social organization. Typically, men must prepare the land for cultivation because there are taboos associated with women operating the plough. Thus, women are never themselves able to initiate the process of cultivating; they must depend on men. Men also own the land, as property among the Hindus of Garhwal is transmitted patrilineally. The labour required to raise crops, however, is almost entirely supplied by women. Women do the planting, weeding and harvesting. There are no "prestige crops", raised exclusively by either sex. Most staple crops are raised by women, provided that men prepare the land by ploughing it for two days in each cropping season.

Government programmes

In almost all the villages, we were told that the various development plans and tribal welfare schemes introduced by the government have failed to make an impact either on the low standard of living in general or on the worsening conditions of women's household drudgery in particular. On the other hand, there are very visible signs of government-initiated development programmes such as those for road construction and the increased number of educational, medical and housing facilities.

In Chamoli district alone, there are sixty-six government intermediate colleges and three postgraduate colleges. The district registered an increase of 52 per cent in literacy in the decade between 1961 and 1971. Although education has begun to have an impact in this region, one old woman in Dewara Kharora village asked me to stop its spread. Because of it, she said, all the educated boys of the village want to go away, leaving women to cope with the harsh life in the hills.

Conversations with local teachers and students gave the impression that development in the form of roads, schools, hospitals, hotels, shops, cinemas, radio and libraries had ensured increased participation on the part of the Garhwal region in the mainstream of national development. One old man stated in a calm voice:

> "Whether we like it or not, the government is opening up this area. For sure, the government is only working in its own selfish interests, and it has no aim of benefiting the people. All the same, it is up to us to benefit from the new developments, and if we want to take advantage of the new schemes we must prepare ourselves to come forward and push the outsiders out."

ORIGINS OF THE CHIPKO MOVEMENT

The Chipko is one of many "people's" ecological movements that have sprung into being over the past ten to twenty years. These movements are fundamentally different from ecological movements in the industrialized world. There, industrial pollution and even "development" are seen as threats, but threats primarily to present lifestyles. In the Chipko movement, however, the basic concern is the very survival of the people in the hill areas. Rather than using the media to try to influence government policies, the people here have had to resort to a popular struggle.

The DGSM

Although the Chipko movement was officially begun on 24 April 1973 by some Sarvodaya workers (all male) at Mandal, Chamoli district, the organizers had already been active in the field of social reconstruction for the previous thirteen years.

One of the movement's leaders, C.P. Bhatt, and his co-workers, who belong to Chamoli district and and had worked for increased employment for local people, believe in the ideology of non-violence as propagated by Mahatma Gandhi and Vinoba Bhave. In 1960, they founded a workers' co-operative which organized unskilled and semi-skilled construction workers. For some time, they worked successfully in this field. One of their schemes, begun in 1964, aimed at creating more employment through the exploitation of the forests. The group established the Dasholi Gram Swarajya Mandal (DGSM) workers' co-operative and entered the market by buying forest rights through auctions to supply its small workshop making farm tools for local use. After initial success, however, the group was outmanoeuvred by other, richer contractors.

In the meantime, the DGSM thought of starting a new enterprise – the collection of roots and herbs from the forest. In this activity, the co-operative gave employment to about 1,000 persons between 1969 and 1972. In 1971 it opened up a small processing plant in Gopeshwar, which manufactured turpentine and resin from pine sap. Again the DGSM had difficulties, this time because the Forestry Department did not allot adequate supplies of pine sap even when the price paid for it was higher than that paid by a partly state-owned producer in the plains. For eight months in 1971–2, the plant had to be closed down for lack of raw material. The plant therefore worked for a total of only four months. The Sarvodaya workers thus faced difficulties with government policies in each of their enterprises.

Demonstrations

On 22 October 1971, villagers from nearby areas demonstrated in Gopeshwar against government forestry policy. Meanwhile, the Forestry Department, which had earlier refused the DGSM's annual request for ten ash trees for its farm-tools workshop, allotted 300 ash trees to the Simon Company, a sporting-goods manufacturer from the plains, thus putting tennis rackets before the plough. In March 1973, the agents of the Simon Company arrived in Gopeshwar to supervise the cutting of the trees. There also arrived the Chipko movement.

On 27 March 1973, at a meeting in Gopeshwar, local people decided not to allow a single tree to be felled by the Simon Company. A month later, DGSM workers and villagers from nearby areas marched out of Gopeshwar to Mandal, beating the drum and singing traditional songs. It was a rally of about a hundred persons. the Simon Company agents and their men retreated from Mandal without felling a single tree. This event had an impact on the Forestry Department, which now offered to let the DGSM have one ash tree if it allowed the Simon Company its full quota. the DGSM refused and the Forestry Department increased its offer to two, then three, five and ten trees – the DGSM's original request. Finally, the Forestry Department had to cancel the Simon Company's permit and the trees were assigned to the DGSM instead.

The Forestry Department also ended the ban on pine sap supplies, but at the same time it allotted the Simon Company a new set of ash trees in the Phata forest in another part of the district. On 20 June 1973, a local leader joined hands with the Savodaya workers and organized a Chipko demonstration in Phata, 80 kilometres away from Gopeshwar. Villagers of Phata and Tarsali kept a vigil on their trees until December, thus starting the long story of the Chipko movement.

Monsoon erosion

Thus far the movement had confined itself to the problems of unemployment among the local people. Earlier, the Sarvodaya workers had organized them in several enterprises. Among these activities was a 1970 relief operation, started when monsoon rains flooded the Alaknanda river and swept away hundreds of homes. During the operation, the workers realized that the chief cause of the flood was soil erosion from the clear-cutting of mountain slopes by the lumber companies. Despite the Forestry Department's policy of planting cleared slopes, the base slopes remained bare. Overgrazing and gathering by villagers also caused the baring of many slopes. Another cause of landslides, the DGSM workers pointed out, was road-building.

In 1973, monsoon rains again brought a spate of floods in the area. By this time, the DGSM had fairly well spelt out its interconnected goals of raising local people's consciousness about the government's forestry policy, about their rights to use the local forest and about their responsibility to preserve the environment through a programme of afforestation. During the 1973 flood-relief operations, the DGSM workers observed the sad plight of the women who had lost their houses, farm and cattle in floods. The series of recurring landslides that followed (1977, 1978, 1979) caused severe damage to life and property, making villagers almost paupers. Working in areas affected by floods and landslides, C.P. Bhatt and his companions heard long stories of suffering by women. This experience gave them both an insight into women's problems and an unprecedented direct contact with them.

Confrontation

When the Forestry Department announced an auction of almost 2,500 trees in the Reni forest overlooking the Alaknanda river, which had flooded in 1970, Bhatt reminded the villagers of the earlier flood and warned of more landslides and more floods if the remaining forests were cut down. He suggested that they hug the trees as a tactic to save them.

Who listened to him? As subsequent events showed, it was women rather than men who got his message. One woman, Gaura Devi, organized the women of her village, Lata, and faced down the workmen of the company that had won the auction for felling the trees. It was a situation that almost forced women to take action – which they did with firmness and unyielding courage. Gaura Devi later described the encounter in graphic detail, commenting on the rude behaviour of some of the men and on how she pushed herself forward in front of the gun of one of these labourers. She challenged the man to shoot her instead of cutting down the trees, comparing the forest with her mother's home (*maika*). Eventually, she and her companions forced the men to retreat.

Following this demonstration of strength by women, the Uttar Pradesh government decided to set up a committee of experts to investigate the situation, and the lumber company withdrew its men from Reni to wait for the committee's decision. The committee, after two years, reported that the Reni forest was an ecologically sensitive area and that no trees should be cut in this region. The government placed a ten-year ban on all tree-felling in an area of over 1,150 square kilometres. This event blazed a trail: at Gopeshwar in June 1975, at Bhyndar valley ("valley of flowers") in January 1978, at Parsari (Joshimath) in August 1979, and at Dongri Paintoli in February 1980, women took the lead in Chipko demonstrations

"The real leaders are the women"

The recent Chipko movement has popularly been referred to as a women's movement, but it is only some male Chipko activists who have been projected into visibility. The women's contribution has been neglected and remains invisible, in spite of the fact that the history of Chipko is a history of the visions and actions of exceptionally courageous women. Environmental movements like Chipko have become historical landmarks because they have been fuelled by the ecological insights and political and moral strengths of women. The experience of these powerful women also needs to be shared to remind us that we are not alone, and that we do not take the first steps: others have walked before us.

The Chipko process as a resurgence of womanpower and ecological concern in the Garhwal Himalaya is a similar mosaic of many events and multiple actors. The significant catalysers of the transformations which made Chipko resistance possible have been women like Mira Behn, Sarala Behn, Bimala Behn, Hima Devi, Gauri Devi, Gunga Devi, Bachni Devi, Itwari Devi, Chamun Devi and many others. The men of the movement, like Sunderlal Bahuguna, Chandi Prasadd Bhatt, Ghanshyam Shailani and Dhoom Singh Negi, have been their students and followers.

In the commemorative column dedicated to Sarala Behn on her seventy-fifth birthday (which coincided with International Women's Year in 1975) the activists of Uttarakhand called her the daughter of the Himalaya and the mother of social activism in the region. Sarala Behn had come to India in search of non-violence. As a close follower of Gandhi, she worked mainly in the hill areas during the independence movement.

She established the Laxmi Ashram in Kausani primarily to empower the hill women. Bimla Behn, who spent seven years with her, widened her project and established the Navjivan Ashram in Silyara, which then became the energizing source for Chipko.

"The real leaders are the women" – continued

The organizational base of women was thus ready by the 1970s, and this decade saw the beginning of more frequent popular protest concerning the rights of the people to utilize local forest produce. 1972 saw widespread, organized protests against the commercial exploitation of forests by outside contractors: in Purola on 11 December, in Uttarkashi on 12 December, and in Gopeshwar on 15 December. It was then that Raturi composed his famous poem:

> Embrace our trees
> Save them from being felled
> The property of our hills
> Save it from being looted.

While the concept of saving trees by embracing them is old, as recalled by the case of the Bishnois, in the context of the current phase of the movement for forest rights, this popular poem is the earliest documentary source of the now-famous name, "Chipko".

The movement spread throughout Garhwal and into Kumaon, through the totally decentred leadership of local women, connected to each other not vertically, but horizontally – through the songs of Ghanshyam Raturi, through "runners" like Bahuguna, Bhatt, and Negi, who carried the message of Chipko happenings from one village to the next, from one region to another. For hill women, food production begins with the forest. Disappearing forests and water are quite clearly an issue of survival for hill women, which is why thousands of Garhwal women have protested against commercial forestry which has destroyed their forests and water resources.

and saved forests from felling. After the Reni success, Bhatt and his workers began to address themselves to women and found them very sensitive and responsive to ecological problems. Women who were never before seen in any of the village meetings were asked to attend. They welcomed this opportunity and turned out in great numbers.

Political involvement

The events at Dongri Paintoli village, according to Bhatt, indicated a new development in the movement. During a meeting between the members (all male) of the village council and the officials of the Horticulture Department for felling. The department, in turn, would provide the villagers with a cement road, a secondary school, a new hospital and electricity for their village. Some DGSM workers, together with Bhatt, tried to explain the implications of development and the importance of conservation. However, the village men, especially the members of the village council, did not agree. They maintained that a school, a hospital, a road and electricity were far more important for the village than a few hundred trees.

Yet the efforts of Bhatt and others did not go to waste on the local women, who decided to hold a Chipko demonstration if anyone tried to fell the trees. They even asked Bhatt and his men to help them. On hearing about this, the members and president of the village council became infuriated at the "outrageous" behaviour of their women. They asked the women to confine themselves to their fields and homes and simultaneously issued a written warning to Bhatt that if he tried to agitate or organize the village women, he would be killed upon arrival at the village.

All this did not deter the women of Dongri Paintoli, and on 9 February 1980 they did not even wait for Bhatt to arrive but turned out in large numbers, held a Chipko demonstration and prevented any tree-felling. Nine days later, the government ordered the forest-felling in that area stopped, and within a month a ban on any further cutting was effected. Subsequently, women leaders in the village were defamed and asked not to attend further meetings.

IMPLICATIONS FOR SOCIETY

The women in Reni took action only because there were no men in the village around to do so. Their "action" was to ask the tree-fellers to wait until their men returned so that some discussion could take place between the two sides (of men) as equals. Women took charge of the scene only in the absence of men, but once they did take charge, they succeeded.

In Dongri Paintoli, by contrast, rather than merely taking a decision in the absence of men, the women stood up against decisions made by their own men. Although they faced opposition from men, they held to their conviction. This certainly marked a major step forward in terms of women's role in the Chipko movement.

In Gopeshwar, women have now formed a co-operative of their own, the Mahila Mandal, to ensure protection of the forest around the town. Its work is carried out regularly by watchwomen, who receive regular wages. Under their supervision, the extraction of forest produce for daily necessities is accomplished in a regulated manner, so as not to harm the trees. Women or men violating these rules are fined, and these fines are deposited in a common fund. Those who do not obey the rules face the punishment of having their tools confiscated. In addition, more and more of the DGSM educational camps are now attended by women, who come despite their busy routines. They take part in discussions and become articulate in expressing their views through this mode of informal education. Their programme, of course, is only in its initial stages. In most villages, women were found to be too busy in their day-to-day tasks to have time for the Chipko meetings and camps.

It can only be said that the cases of Reni and Dongri Paintoli and the organization of women into the Mahila Mandal at Gopeshwar are indicative of the latent potentialities in the organization and mobilization of resources by women whose consciousness has been raised. A situational analysis of the crisis periods shows how village women work in handling their problems: when new ideas and methods of handling problems are introduced by leaders, they are quick to act.

Disagreement on development

The situational conflicts in Chamoli district arose because of the different meanings attached to the word "development" by different groups of people. Men, who sit on village councils and other village bodies and head their families, view the government officials with a great deal of respect and fear. They dare not oppose them. Women, on the other hand, who have never had any contact with government officials or other outsiders, have no model of interaction to follow with them. The Chamoli women understood only that the felling of trees is harmful to their well-being, and they simply acted according to that belief. On the basis of their past interaction with government officials, men are convinced of the great powers of the government. they consider it wrong to oppose its policies.

We have a situation where female energy – at least up until now – is concentrated in the subsistence, reproductive and nurturing spheres and male energy is concentrated in public power and authority. Now, with more paid jobs available to men in construction and other labouring sectors, they are not so dependent upon women for their subsistence needs. These changes are causing a reformulation of traditional relationships between the sexes in these villages.

Women's participation in the Chipko movement, however limited in numbers or in its impact on the general way of life, has implications for possible changes in gender relationships in the Garhwali society. One Chipko village leader summarized the present situation of the movement by saying that, at present, 90 per cent of women and 10 per cent of men are with him, while 90 per cent of men and 10 per cent of women oppose him. He considers that only through non-violent methods will the movement win over the other men.

What we read about women's participation in the movement and what its leaders talk about are simplified and idealized images of reality. This idealization has, in turn, led to an unrealistic belief that the participation of women in the development process can be achieved by a mere ideological commitment and a few organizational devices. The account given here demonstrates that the release of spontaneity and creativity on the part of rural women in Garhwal is chiefly a by-product of actions initiated at the grass-roots level by the Sarvodaya workers to increase people's awareness about the environment. At present, these workers and their leaders face the problem of handling an unforeseen release of woman-power in this area.

Ecological balance is an important aspect of new approaches to development, and women's concern with local ecological problems is vital. In a majority of existing programmes for women's development, the top–down approach is used. Decision-making, evaluation and control rest at the top with planners and policy-makers, while participants lack the scope to develop their own skills or to have any political say in deciding their own affairs. If we aspire to change in the social and political situation of women, we have to look at alternative approaches to replace the traditional power structure; hence the need to study women's participation in social movements.

Even the supporters of the Chipko movement and its leaders are not free from traditional constraints. In home and family situations, egalitarianism is almost absent and there are invariably tensions and inequalities which have implications for the stratification system of the society as a whole. The relevant questions are:

- Is it possible that only a few instances of the successful exercise of power by women can lead to further demands for sharing power in both public and private?
- Are women able to face opposition from men, and for how long?
- Does coercion by men alienate women from their families, or does there come about another pattern of relationship between the sexes?

These questions cannot be answered right now. As the Chipko movement is still in its infancy, we have to observe further developments and observe what happens to the role of women within it.

REFERENCES

Joshi, G., "Forest Policy and Tribal Development", *Social Action*, 31: 446–468 (1981).

Lancaster, C.S., "Women, Horticulture and Society in Sub-Saharan Africa", *Am. Anthrop.*, 539-564 (1978).

Middleton, C., "Sexual Inequality and Stratification Theory", in F. Parkin (ed.), *The Social Analysis of Class Structure* (London: Tavistock, 1971), pp. 179–203.

Minault, G., *The Extended Family: Women and Political participation in India and Pakistan* (Delhi: Chanakya Publications, 1981).

Mitra, S., "Ecology as Science and Science Fiction", *Econ. & Political Wkly*, 17:147–152 (1982).

Seacombe, W., "The Housewife and Her Labour under Capitalism", *New Left Rev.*, 83:3–24 (1971).

8

THE BANKURA STORY: RURAL WOMEN ORGANIZE FOR CHANGE
Nalini Singh

In a small village in West Bengal, a women's Samity (society) obtained land donation in 1980 from private landowners who lacked the resources to develop the degraded land. With unwavering focus, and collective will, the Samity reclaimed the wasteland, and in three years the land was thick with trees on which tassar silkworms are reared. As news spread, other Samities were formed by women in surrounding villages, each with land donation from villagers, and today 1,500 women in thirty-six villages are members of such Samities. The groups have also organized supplementary income-generating activities, on an individual or group basis.

Samity members can now survive without four-yearly migrations to distant districts in search of work because they have created employment for themselves by expanding the productive base of the local economy. Women's bargaining power as workers has increased because of their link with an asset-owning Samity. There is a new confidence amongst the members that they can influence the course of their own lives through the Samities, where "all are responsible for all".

The Samities have been supported by the Centre for Women's Development Studies (CWDS, New Delhi), and ILO's Programme for Rural Women (New Delhi). These organizations have provided technical guidance and counsel, and catalytic funding. Government schemes have emerged as the major source of funding.

POOREST RURAL WOMEN AS COLLEAGUES

"Everybody thinks this land is useless," says Jilapi, "but now its colour will change from brown to emerald."

The women nod agreement, as if they share a deep faith and trees will survive on the poor soil with care and skill, and without interference from families. Women are elated that their degraded family land has been donated to the Samity.

Chandmuni is quiet, and then a smile struggles to the surface through the heavy impasto of airless years. "When I proposed the transfer of our land to the Samity, my husband said, "If a women's group can make this useless land fertile, how can I object? After all the women belong to the village, so our households will benefit."

But that is not true. The Samity's rule is: no land-donor has more right to employment or output of the land, because all members have an equal share. Landless women, with nothing to donate, have joined the Samity, as also have women from other villages. An exceptional situation has arisen, where a few poor women are both benefactors and beneficiaries of land donation, but the benefit also extends to assetless and other women who couldn't donate anything.

Jhilimili lies in West Bengal's Bankura district. This area is a wide swath of rolling hills, with overexploited land and water resources. Once the district had thick mixed forests of *sal*, *neem*, *kendu*. "Then my breakfast was in the forests," recalls eighty-year-old Kali, "berries and honey."

Santhal tribals lost their wooded land to settlers from the plains. Traders, cultivators and contractors saw in the forests the basis for supplying cities and "developing" pockets with timber, forest products, and later, agricultural produce from cleared patches.

Most tribals sold or pledged their land in return for a few sacks of grain. The loss of private lands was a keen setback, but possibly a greater loss was the disappearance of forests which were their natural habitat, and their life-support system.

This part of Bankura district provided few opportunities for wage labour, so survival depended on migration to private farms in neighbouring Hoogly (200 km) and Burdwan (150 km). Even today, in several parts of Bankura district, migratory wage labour is the primary source of income. Government's ongoing employment programmes together generate about three weeks' work for rural workers. But they need work for twelve months!

"*Namal* [migration] is very harsh. We earned Rs. 5 for fourteen hours' work on the *jotedar's* [big cultivators] paddy wetlands. Two of my daughters died from exposure," Chandmuni grieves quietly. "When we returned, we found that our houses had collapsed and we had to start all over again."

To be assetless, unemployed, illiterate, destitute, yet overworked, tired and weak: this defines the state of most rural women in India. Bankura's landless women exist a whole lifetime in that category, practising *ad hoc* methods of survival, each to herself. Yet even in this pattern of individual survival, there are some traces of the collective Santhal tradition. Today, too, community members make group ritual offerings in the forest, women collect minor forest products in groups, and families live in a close cluster of hamlets. Tribal women despair only when food stocks are exhausted. At other times their natural optimism convinces them that better times lie ahead, and they wait.

With the waiting, Badani has lost some of the strength of her limbs, but she has kept the madness of her heart intact. "I talk boldly, so outsiders used to call me mad, but nobody called me mad when I told them the truth about the meeting in Jhilimili in 1980."

She refers to the meeting of women agricultural labourers in Jhilimili village in 1980, convened by Benoy Chowdhry, West Bengal's Minister for Land Reforms, who was worried about women's poor showing in Barga operation for determining inheritance rights of sharecroppers, distribution of homesteads and institutional credit.

Badani told the Minister, "We have been losing our forests, which gave us food, fodder, fuel and a livelihood. Today, we have too little work here, and have to go on *namal*. Why don't you give land to women? Are we not peasants? Why are homesteads not in our name? How do we protect the children when our men throw us out?"

"But you don't depend on your men to feed you, you have worked all your life," said the Minister. "Why do you allow them to treat you that way?"

"We have to because we don't have enough work, and we are powerless. We can deal with them if we are strong and organized. Can't you give us work locally? Then we can organize."

Officials noted the proceedings, but couldn't find a category or government scheme which could capitalize on women's optimism and determination.

"Let us train them in bee-keeping and tailoring. But collective action and enterprise? Who will motivate, who will supervise? Who will maintain accounts? These are all illiterate women."

Generalizations have their usual failings, but the Jhilimili meeting pointed to a few common experiences: women have been systematically deprived of control over land, both private and common land, and this has reduced productive employment for women, and eroded their bargaining power. All women want work locally. They recognize more than men that regenerative powers of nature are limited, and they are more sensitive to the intricate relationships that link living organisms to their environment. Not surprisingly, women resent eucalyptus plantations on common lands by the Forestry Department: "You think of a tree as a piece of dead wood. For us it is living. It gives us fruit, fuelwood, fodder and shade. We care for a tree like our own child. Only when our stomachs are empty would we think of cutting a tree."

Present at the Jhilimili meeting, at government invitation, were representatives of the Delhi-based research organization, the Centre for Women's Development Studies (CWDS). "While the women's voices rose in honest description of their problems, I was asked by the Minister to stay back and ensure that government action was imaginative enough to enable the women to work collectively," says Vina Mazumder, CWDS Director.

But there was the inevitable question: "It is feasible for a research organization to get involved in active implementation? Is it valid for outsiders, since we are based 1,000 kilometres away?" argued some members of CWDS. Other colleagues debated: "But wouldn't such a project give a chance to CWDS to demonstrate that economic activity *can* be a catalyst for women's organizations to become empowered? Anyway, how does one withdraw in the face of such need?"

Anticipating some action by CWDS, women from three villages in Bankura's Ranibandh block[1] bunched together in informal clusters.

CWDS representatives registered them as *Gramin Mahila Saramil Unayan Samiti*[2] (GMSUS), one organization each for the village clusters of Bhurkura, Jhilimili and Chendapather.

"Then we talked to the women about elections and democratic decision-making." Duly again, the women voted, and some leaders as well as some figureheads were elected as Executive Committee members.

What activities would the Samities start? They had decided not to go on *namal*. Work was necessary immediately. The women said, "This is the season for collecting *kendu* leaves and *sal* seeds. Will the government buy from us at a fair price? The *Mantri* [Minister] led our movement for a fair price for kendu leaves in 1976. Won't he help now he is the *Sarkar*?" The *Sarkar* did, by ordering the local co-operative (LAMPS) to give an agency to the Samiti. The Samities began to organize the collection and sale of kendu leaves and sal seeds from the forest.

Samity members and CWDS organizers realized that unless the women were represented on the local bodies they would be neglected. Two of the Samities became affiliated to the West Bengal Tribal Development Co-operative Corporation (WBTDCC), and gained access to the local LAMPS (Large Multipurpose Co-operative Society), which trades in forest produce.

Even as the news of the seed collection in Jhilimili rolled over the hills to Bhurkura, news travelled from there that private land had been donated by the villagers for plantation with arjun and asan, the host plants of the tassar silkworm. Rearing of tassar cocoons in the forests is a traditional occupation and the land would be used by the Samity for cocoon production.

"Incredible, I thought," says CWDS Project Co-ordinator in Bankura, N. Banerjee (Narayan). "There it was, a consolidated chunk of nine acres. The Bhurkura Samity women smiled, even those who had donated land, and I thought, 'At this level of poverty, perhaps only a group can ensure survival of individuals.'"

Emotions are important in an innovative endeavour because they mirror the human trauma which accompanies change. In Bhurkura, very poor families gave away their land to an untested Samity, while landless women began to experience asset-holding for the first time.

Says an organizer. "Their attachment to the land grew. They started visiting the plot and planning its use."

Member Gouri explains, "I earn about Rs. 200 from tassar cocoon rearing on the land which used to belong to my family, but is now the Samity's. But I also experience some security from Kamala's earning of about Rs. 200. She is landless, and each year her family went without daily meals in January and June. Their hunger cut into our insides too. It is not easy to live with your neighbour's hunger."

WOMEN RECLAIM WASTELANDS

How was the Bhurkura patch to be planted? CWDS contacted the local Forest Ranger, and he provided arjun and asan saplings to the Bhurkura Samity. Organizers also transported saplings from distant Birbhum (250 km), where the Forestry Department raised nurseries. The Tribal Welfare Department of the government of West Bengal sanctioned a grant of Rs. 100,000 for the plantation. Men cleared the land, women planted the saplings. Each activity was accompanied by discussion: "Who will rear the worms?" "How will wages be decided?" "Who will buy the cocoons?" Emphasizes a CWDS team member, "There was unprecedented enthusiasm and faith in the Samities."

While Bhurkura debated and pondered these question. Jhilimili and Chendapather Samities also received land donations of about 10 acres each from their villages. To mobilize resources for plantation work and to invite Ministers to the Samities training camp in 1982, the CWDS staff started the trek back to the district headquarters, and Calcutta. A few Samity members travelled with them.

Writers' Building, the secretariat complex, was the venue of their meeting with the Chief Minister and the Minister for Land and Land Reforms, and Panchayat and Rural Development. These meetings did not establish unhindered access to state funds, but strengthened the Samities' claim to various schemes.

CWDS explains: "We discovered that government funds are frittered away in a thousand schemes, and it requires entrepreneurial perseverance to gain knowledge and access to them. Of course, the state authorities were more convinced of the Samities' claim when they met the members. And the members got the crucial message that if you demand collectively, government supports you."

The 1982 camp gave a boost to sanction and release of government funds, especially via the local Panchayat Samiti. A rough count shows that in a one-year period, twelve government schemes were tapped for funding the activities of the three Samities. Grants ranged from Rs. 500 to Rs. 396,000.

Government funds met the labour and plantation costs and part of the maintenance costs. Women then volunteered their labour to protect and maintain the plants, organizing themselves into village-based groups with a group leader.

With the plants, the spirit grew: "The plants dotted our red hills, and we felt secure because these plants were not the property of the Forestry Department or the Panchayat or village households. Their future depended on us, and on the decisions we made together.

"We understood that if we didn't tend the saplings, the whole effort of coming together would be a waste. And wasted effort is a luxury for us." At starvation point you don't neglect the lifeline.

Plant survival has been routinely 98 per cent on the Samities' plantations, a striking contrast to the average survival rate of 55 per cent on plantations undertaken by government departments in other parts of the country. Also, the plants were ready for rearing worms in the second year, a full eighteen months before normal gestation!

Back at Bhurkura and Jhilimili, the plantations had a steady stream of official and other visitors. They were impressed, and offered training facilities in tassar rearing at the Central Silk Board's field station at Birbhum. This Centre was also directed to supply silkworm eggs (disease-free layings) to the Samity, and thus rearing started in twenty-four months. Women organized a job-sharing roster for three crops reared during the rearing period, July to January.

The first batch of cocoons was sold to the Department of Sericulture, which has remained the major client. Women produce high-quality seed cocoons.

EMPLOYMENT BEGINS TO DIVERSIFY

Then the Samities decided to diversify to other income-earning activities which matched the women's needs and skills, were based on local demand, and used local raw materials such as sal tree leaves.

Broad-leaved sal trees have been used traditionally to make leaf-cups and plates, and the Chendapather Samity pioneered production of the upgraded sal leaf "tableware", with polythene lining. Women learnt machine operations and repair of equipment eagerly.

The EC (Executive Committee) fixed the daily wage on the basis of the prescribed minimum wage, and not on the costing of manufacture of sal plates! But who would operate the machines, and enjoy a steady income?

"Nobody," came the Samity's decision, "We will work in half-day shifts at Rs. 3 a shift and rotate the women members once a fortnight on shifts." This chain-assembly method provided a fortnight's assured part-time work to fifty women on eight machines, about five times as many as would have been benefited from the one-women-per-machine norm. WBTDCC offered cash credit at 4 per cent interest to Jhilimili and Chendapather Samities, and the Tribal Welfare Department provided a grant of about Rs. 50,000 for the purchase of machines.

Says Balika, "My earnings from plate-making are Rs. 56 a month. Add to this Rs. 50 for the other fortnight when I get some work in agriculture or as road coolie, and I have a living wage in the village."

All these ventures are based on collective management and income-sharing, which are thorny concepts under ordinary conditions, more so under conditions of privation. Differences *have* arisen, but the women have handled them pragmatically, and prevented them from grounding the units, with help from the CWDS staff. "The enterprises are not only businesses, they have become an expression of women's self-worth, so they guard against disruption," observes a CWDS organizer.

"This income is a little different to income from normal work," analyses Rashi, "because here I am part of the discussions, and know what is going on in the business, whether work will be available next month or not. This makes me secure, there is more certainty, even if there is not a full month's work."

Diversification continued. The Samities' activities expanded. Rope-making from golden stalks of the local babui grass was introduced in Jhilimili, and the Samity also started trading in mahua seeds, buying them from members in the flush season and selling them back later to the same women at prices which are well below market rates, but at a marginal profit to the Samity. Under another scheme, individual women have received advance from the Samity of Rs. 200 each for purchase of paddy for rice-husking. This activity generates enough rice, in service charges, to meet home consumption needs.

Today women have started, or are discussing, several other employment activities: dairying based on cultivation of fodder grasses on Samities' plots. Yorkshire breed pig-raising. Khaki Campbell duckery, mahua seed collection, handmade paper from babui grass, nurseries for forest plantations, vegetable cultivation, lac articles, bone digester units, tassar spinning and weaving, rice-husking, soap-making, tailoring, small shop for local needs, and rabbit-rearing.

The mosaic of activities defines the entrepreneurial zeal of the Samity members, who have blended old skills with updated technology.

But not all income-generating activities of the Samities have been successful. Minor livestock such as goats, pig, and poultry were the women's natural choice as subsidiary occupation, but inclination alone did not guarantee success, as in poultry.

The government hatchery at Durgapur (150 km away) agreed to supply day-old chicks to the Jhilimili and Bhurkura Samities. A few Samity members and the CWDS Project Director hired a tempo and thundered down the highway in high spirits, squatting on the floor of the vehicle. Since the hatchery lacks training facilities, its poultry experts gave only cursory instructions, and sent off the chicks, members and staff in a hurry.

"On the way back I sensed our suppressed excitement: somewhere the adrenalin was flowing!" remembers Narayan.

But the performance of the poultry units varied. At Chendapather the venture failed because chicken-feed had to be brought from a distance of 60 km, an unforeseen problem. Where CWDS organizers supervised closely, as at Jhilimili, the experiment was a moderate success.

The Samities reviewed the unsatisfactory record, and changed policy. Day-old chicks were purchased again, transported carefully, and reared for seventy-five days by selected paid members, emphasizing the local scavenging feed mix. Grown chicks were supplied to selected members against a loan of Rs. 44.75 for six chicks. The hens proved to be good layers, and although poultry experts adjudge the activities as inefficiently labour-intensive, women themselves regard it as "very economic". But the Chendapather Samity abandoned poultry, and switched to goat-rearing.

"Women members are most responsible borrowers," remarks a CWDS staffer. "Half the women repaid the loan within six months."

TRAINING FOR MOBILIZATION
AND ENTREPRENEURSHIP

"Illiterate women are not ignorant." This single belief led the CWDS staff to stress training for the Samity members.

Particularly, the economics of these small businesses were precarious in the earlier stages. So CWDS decided to focus on professional management training for the women.

Abhijit Dasgupta is a professional management consultant experienced in the corporate sector, male, city-dweller with seemingly all the wrong qualifications for training rural women in management. But he was interested, spoke Bangla and had earlier advised CWDS on marketing leaf plates. He was recruited.

"I held a five-day management training course in Jhilimili, the first in my life with rural illiterate women. Five women leaders from each of the three Samities attended, about fifteen women in all. The first thing I learnt was that these trainees were more serious about learning than almost any batch I could remember.

"We discussed specific questions: What is a Samity? A member's role? What is an enterprise? Profit and loss? With equity and justice? How is responsibility shared? How is work shared in an organization? What is the role of a *Sardar* [leader]? How is a plan of action devised, and handed over from one shift to another? And of course, financial management and maintenance of accounts."

The women could not follow management techniques easily, but they were resolute learners. Simple management practices soon became *derigueur* in the structure of the Samities. Management training workshops were repeated every quarter for a year with the same women, and the group got bigger each time as more members felt they must attend.

Training is regarded by CWDS organizers as a means of human-resource development, but equally as a mobilizing technique. It is significant that the most ardent trainees are deserted young women, widows, childless oppressed wives, whose need for affiliation and support is highest.

Says Vinadi, "Wage labour displays a psychology of dependence on work-givers. This is reflected in their language. The psychology of entrepreneurship and self-reliance represents a tremendous transition and challenge to these women." Therefore CWDS considers that women need continuous training in management of assets, enterprise, and organization-building.

"We hold rural training workshops, and the fact of living together for a few days, without distinction of village, occupation or age, is memorable because it binds different women together. There is ruthless criticism, as well as warmth, and understanding of the personal and the professional," says and EC member.

The GMSUS training workshops are attended by representatives of other Samities. Some formal vocation-related training sessions are conducted, but generally workshops focus on policy issues. Are Samities' assets heritable? Who can succeed a member? Can Samities challenge dowry, alcoholism? Countless questions are debated, new ideas thrive, the agenda is improvised and revised.

For professional and occupation-related skills, CWDS organizers have mobilized ongoing government training programmes (e.g. twenty women a year are trained by government in silk-rearing), or have invited consultants such as AFPRO[3] for subject-specific training courses. Often women identify training needs – as, for instance, in legal rights. Now the women train new members, and trainees from other districts.

CWDS is realistic about the time required for meaningful transfer of skills, and emphasizes continuous training.

Rigorous training has led to multiple gains – women are active participants in management, and they have acquired technical skills for regeneration of wasted community assets. They are now expert trainers. When CWDS was asked by the government of India to train its own officers on rural women's development issues, it accepted the challenge on condition that the real trainers would be the GMSUS women.

Through women's mobilizing and technical skills, non-productive land has been reclaimed, and returned to the productive system as an economic resource. This is the first initiative by the community against ecological degradation.

In Ranibandh and Khatra blocks, over a period of seven years, 250 acres (10 hectares) of wasteland have been reclaimed, and today these lands are being exploited scientifically to yield an average income of Rs. 7,000 per hectare in tassar worm rearing, babui grass cultivation-cum-rope-making, etc.

Ecological gains are impressive: these hill slopes have a green cover, which has reversed the process of sheet erosion, and revegetation has assisted groundwater recharge. On an ecological audit alone the cost-benefit ratio is heavily loaded in favour of the Samities' initiative.

HOW IS THE MOVEMENT SPREADING?

"No change takes place simply through the infusion of capital. Change occurs if there's a movement around something that appeals to people. Then, it spreads quickly," observed Minister Benoy Choudhury about the population of the Samities. "Can this Bankura women's model spread to other districts with similar problems, Purulia and Medinipur?" he asked in 1983.

By then the women had already started sharing the "model" with others, and today the Samities have an important inbuilt resource – a spearhead team. This team is constituted of some of the oldest members of the Samities. The team is self-selected, and acts as a front-rank consciousness-raising and advisory group.

One day a daughter of Bhurkura, who is married in Baroghotu village in the adjoining Khatra block, told her in-laws about women in her natal village, who had greened a hillside, and about those earning a living wage from such efforts. The villagers took a spot decision to start the same process in their village, and asked the young woman for more information. She contacted her mother at Bhurkura.

"Who will teach the other villagers?" the mother wondered. "So we contacted women leaders from Jhilimili, discussed the matter, and a few of us visited Baroghotu village. We explained the benefits and problems, and told the women to look for land."

This was the birth of the spearhead team. Since then the team has counselled, motivated and supported several other groups which want to replicate the Bhurkura experience.

Recalling the spearhead team's exertions on behalf of the women in Khatra block, Narayan says, "The women shamed me into visiting Baroghotu, which I was avoiding because of doubts about our handling capacity. When I saw the 40-acre hillock pledged by the village community to a future Samity, I was appalled. The land was red laterite, in a severe stage of erosion, with quartzite outcroppings.

"Nothing will grow here," pronounced the sericulture expert. On the way back I walked through the hamlet. Many naked, half-fed children with diseased skin came out. They were not washed because mothers had no time. Women looked famished. They spoke little, but when they did, it was in despair: 'This hillock *can* give us income, we want to plant it, you must help us.'"

Narayan considered the expert's advice: "Don't do it".

"So I did it, took the risk." The women's need and motivation were transparent.

Women prepared the entire patch for planting within fifteen days. The Forestry Department supplied only 30,000 saplings, whereas 100,000 pits were prepared. "But it was a beginning. We had a good monsoon, and the saplings were a metre high by the next season."

Success of the first few Samities was a powerful stimulant, and women from other villages grouped and regrouped. There were a few false starts. For instance, residents of Kumharpara village in the Ranibandh area approached the CWDS staff, agreed to the land transfer, but then fell out over the question of abdication of ownership to the Samity. Later they decided again to donate land, and formed a Samity.

From experience the spearhead team organizers had realized that the registration of the Samity and the land must go together. "I told the men clearly: no land, no Samity," says Narayan, "Of course you might say that this was arm-twisting, but that's what we said."

Each new Samity started with a small land donation. Soon they had obtained more land gifts. The new Samities also had a basket of supplementary income-generating activities for women.

At the end of 1984 – that is, three years after the project started – there were three registered Samities. By early 1988, the number had grown to twelve Samities in two blocks of the district and Purulia with a total membership of 1,500 women. The thirteenth Samity is on the verge of registration. Membership of individual Samities ranges from 30 to 500. New Samities have fewer members (30 to 50) and are localized around one or two villages.

Each Samity is clearly a mobilizing and participatory mechanism, quite distinct from a grass-roots organization which is a link in any delivery mechanism. Claims cwds, "The Samities provide a model of the organizational structure which ensures that programmes actually reach poor rural women."

SAMITIES AS STRUCTURES OF PARTICIPATION

Structurally, the Samities are organized into the three-tier frame. Each village has ordinary members, who elect a village Executive Committee (EC). EC members from two to three villages constitute the EC of the registered Samity. Each Samity nominates two or three EC members to the apex organization, the Nari Bikash Sangh (NBS), which shapes general policy (see figure).

The principles of election have been understood clearly by the members, and ECs are elected at the village, Samity and apex level for two-year terms. Members try for a consensus, but do not force it. However, sometimes "consensus ECs" are removed *en bloc*, as in Barughotu, where members expressed their lack of confidence by defeating all the old EC members in the last election.

The Samity is the central implementing unit in any village cluster. It plans activities, handles finances and keeps accounts, maintains records of meetings and visitors, liaises with local government officials and with the Panchayat[4] and Panchayat Samity,[5] organizes general body

ORGANIZATIONAL STRUCTURE

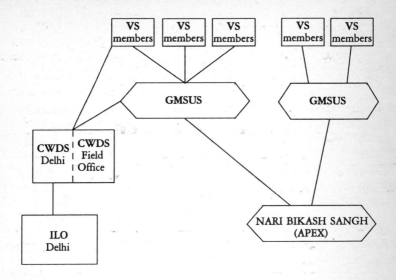

VS: Village Samity with a nominated Executive Committee (EC)
GMSUS: Gramin Mahila Shramik Unnayan Samity with an elected EC
(Rural Women Workers' Advancement Society)
Nari Bikash Sangh (APEX): Apex organization, constituted of
representatives of GMSUS, also with an elected EC (Woman's Advance-
ment Union)
CWDS: Centre for Women's Development Studies, New Delhi
ILO: International Labour Organization Programme for Rural Women,
New Delhi

Growth at a glance		
	1981	1988
No. of registered Samities	3	13
No. of members	400	1,500
Hectares reclaimed for Arjun plantation	3	100
Person-days of direct employment generated	18,000	36,000

meetings, and responds to requests from other groups-in-the-making.

Regular meetings are emphasized, and are almost institutionalized in the "Bankura experience". The general body of each Samity meets at least once a year, with an attendance of at least two-thirds of the membership, which is a quorum. Some NBS members are present Personal experience of members' work on the plantations or sal plate machines, goats, etc., are exchanged, and where additional training or changes are necessary, general policy recommendations are made to the NBS. Sometimes the NBS has to resolve disputes.

Village groups and Samity EC meet once a month, and about fifteen women attend. Often CWDS organizers are present. Discussion includes work-related questions, social forestry and legal implications, small savings and thrift, health and immunization, adult education, study tour reports, and socio-legal issues such as dowry, alcoholism and wife-beating. Individual problems are discussed for instance, grazing the goats of a member who is ill.

ECs of Samities also hold occasional meetings at the Jhilimili "headquarters", the village where the first group came together. They focus on internal management of the project, review physical and social progress. Such meetings are attended by ten to twelve members.

The apex, Nan Bikash Sangh, meets about four times a year. Local problems common to women's lives are discussed for instance, raising the prevailing wage to the minimum wage rate. The apex also maintains contact with women's groups from Orissa and Bihar, and representatives of these "outside" agencies are invited for exchange and dialogue. The apex manages the small savings of all the Samities, at members' request.

What is the monitoring mechanism in the project? Samity members are keen critics of their own performance, and demand explanations for lapses at the meetings of the General Body, and at the EC meetings at the Samity and apex levels.

If a Samity has been negligent – say in caring for silkworm larvae in the plantations – and the cocoon harvest is lost, all other Samities condemn the lax management in scathing terms: "You are irresponsible. You have let everybody down. Hand over to us." Better performance usually follows.

If a member has absented herself from meetings continuously, other members might ask for an explanation. The defaulting member might retort, "Why should I attend? Only two or three of you decide everything." CWDS staff present at the meeting take serious note of this statement and corrective measures are taken after a full discussion. The monitoring mechanism is largely a system of qualitative self-observation by the members, assisted by CWDS staff and ILO experts who visit the project regularly.

Conventional progress reports are also generated within the project by CWDS staff for each Samity, both monthly and six-monthly. Physical progress is monitored, as well as some indices of human-resource development, such as women's ability to discuss matters with local officials. These reports are forwarded from the Samity to local headquarters, and then to Delhi. At each stage the reports lose details, but the essential thrust to monitor genuine "advancement" remains intact.

SAMITIES, CWDS AND ILO

CWDS Director Vina Mazumdar is Joint Secretary of each of the registered GMSUS. Members thought this prudent to enable CWDS to negotiate with government on their behalf.

Is CWDS strictly an implementing agency, a policy-shaping body, trouble-shooter, bulwark or friend? Its role has attracted much attention as the pivot of the project. Some say it is remarkable but not replicable; others state that CWDS support has been interventionist. What is the role, and has it changed over seven years?

CWDS is an institution with special skills and commitment to human growth and development. At the beginning, CWDS looked upon its function as assisting the women to organize for employment. It selected the instrument of women's Samities for generating employment, and gradually linked wasteland development to women's work. Perhaps for the first time women have participated systematically in the important sectors of land-use planning and soil conservation, thereby changing both the common and the private environment. CWDS then saw collective employment as a means to achieve solidarity, but the ultimate end was women's empowerment. Primarily a research institution, CWDS relied on intensive research in the early stages to derive policy for the project, and then to identify training needs.

For the Samities women, the presence of CWDS is "like a safety net of advice and good counsel". They also regard CWDS as an advocate of the women's viewpoint. CWDS is the women's conduit for contact with the state and central government agencies. In practical terms CWDS has procured for them sound advice on management techniques and financial and technical aspects of activities. CWDS has ensured that ECs and staff have frequent exchanges with the local Panchayat,[4] Ranibandh Panchayat Samity, the Zila Parishad,[5] and the bureaucracy at each level. This contact has persuaded local bodies to recognize women's aspirations, and to assist them in their efforts.

Samity members are now star invitees at local meetings and workshops organized by the block authorities or the elected bodies as at Gramin Melas,[6] inauguration of Kisan Nursery,[7] prize distribution, or even political meetings.

Vinadi provides the philosophical frame of CWDS's role: "So far the process of development has been one in which the women are dispensable. The task is to wrest from society the rights, dignity and resources women are entitled to. This calls for protest against economic and social injustice."

CWDS personnel have no professional background in social forestry, tassar silkworm rearing, or business enterprise. Yet they are not handicapped, because they have attended short training programmes, and their own expertise in human-resource development equips them to identify and mobilize technical inputs. Their concern is to develop effective methods for enhancing women's skills and self-confidence.

The CWDS team is led by Vinadi (she is Delhi-based, and advises through "remote sensing" and frequent visits) and a six-member team based in Jhilimili – the Project Co-ordinator, tassar silk specialist, livestock expert, animator for adult education and supervision of crèches, liaison officer with special duties to work with the block machinery, and accountant. While only two of the team members are female, the women Samity members accept the male extension workers, not only because they are technically qualified but also because the men have displayed a high regard for the women's efforts. Technical consultants are hired periodically for specific purposes.

CWDS invited ILO to participate in this endeavour in its capacity as an international organization with a mandate to support workers' organizations, particularly disadvantaged workers such as women. ILO was interested because one of its basic objectives in technical co-operation is human development by mobilizing resources, not only government, but also private and NGO resources. The project also promised to enrich the resource base of the area, support a higher level of economic activity and create additional local employment.

"Our team has to be maintained in Ranibandh. Can ILO help?" enquired CWDS in 1980.

ILO responded positively in 1981, and through a flexible Aid Fund it supported CWDS staff in Jhilimili and provided assistance for transport, technical consultancy, training of all kinds, experimental activities, and gap-filling in necessary budget items. The Dutch government gave financial support through the ILO under a multi-bilateral project, initially for a three-year period, later extended for another three years (together covering the period 1981–88). A major evaluation is proposed for late 1988. DANIDA[8] is providing assistance through ILO starting in 1988 for extending activities to adjoining districts.

"Gap-filling" emerged as a major back-stopping aid and covered an assortment of expenses such as land registration fees, support to CWDS to appoint a consultant for marketing, purchase of jeep and motorcycle for staff mobility in Ranibandh and Khatra block villages, rental of the CWDS field office, lighting bills, secretariat assistance, etc. This assistance enabled CWDS and the Samities to tap government funds and support by mobilizing major poverty-alleviation schemes as well as routine development programmes.

ILO's support to CWDS for the Samities was derived from Convention 141, which provides the framework for co-operation with rural unorganized workers. India was one of the first countries in Asia to ratify the Convention. The Convention states: "All categories of rural workers, whether they are wage-earners or self-employed, shall have the right to establish and join organizations of their choosing without previous authorization." It further affirms that "Steps shall be taken to promote the widest possible understanding of the need to further the development of rural workers' organizations and of the contribution they can make to increasing employment opportunities."

The association with ILO has linked the women's Samities to the international labour movement. ILO has long regarded unorganized workers, including groups of women workers, as constituents of potential trade unions. So the link-up of the Samities and ILO could shape the Samities' emergence as a trade-union type of organization of rural women workers, who have succeeded in generating employment for themselves by reclaiming degraded natural resources, and by establishing other income-generation activities.

"Since ILO promotes and maintains ties with *shramiks* [workers through their organizations] we consider that our most important function in this case has been to provide technical support to the Samities," says Andrea Singh, Chief Technical Adviser, Programme for Rural Women, ILO's Area Office, New Delhi. "We have provided documentation to them on technical subjects and organizational issues, and supported their training as workers and group members, and simply talked to them about women's achievements in other projects."

During the last several years ILO has maintained a regular flow of information to the Samities and CWDS field staff. The ILO team has also established an informal, organic evaluation system through lively interaction of its consultants and programme staff with Samity members, amd extension workers. ILO's participation in the project stems from its close identification with Samity members' quest for work and dignity.

How much has the Bankura project cost in terms of donor funding? ILO's total project costs in the period 1981–8 have been $350,000. Is this project outlay excessive, or is it modest? To answer, one must apply relevant cost-benefit criteria. But in this case the question is: which criteria are relevant?

At a conventional input–output level, it could be claimed that the project has generated part-time permanent employment for 1,500 women directly on degraded land which had fallen into disuse. Of these women, about 500 have also initiated supplementary

THE BANKURA STORY: RURAL WOMEN ORGANIZE FOR CHANGE

income generation via various activities which they manage themselves. So 1,500 rural families have some more cash, and children's nutrition is just a little better.

Also, 100 hectares of wasteland have been reclaimed, an asset which is currently valued at Rs. 5.0 million (about $385,000). The land yields a gross income of about Rs. 7,000 per hectare in a year's harvest of tassar cocoons. Soil erosion has been prevented – an ecological gain for the community.

But how do you impute a value to women's gain in status within the family and community, emergence of leadership amongst poorest women, their enhanced political participation? Can any index measure adequately the confidence of migrant rural women workers who can now negotiate a floor wage, and exercise the option to stay back in the village? Is it possible to assess a landless woman's sense of security that comes from being a decision-making member of a group that owns productive land? How do you gauge the power experiences by marginalized women, when they quiz the Block Department Officer on their share of provisions for weaker sections?

Perhaps qualitative gains are best described by Samity members, and the CWDS and ILO teams.

Samity member: "Now that we have achieved something, we have courage. . . . Our common fund or asset is our plantation, which we must maintain. . . . Speak and don't hesitate even if you say the wrong thing."

CWDS field organizer: "Women members say that even if the Samity were to offer no financial gain, they'd still hold meetings."

CWDS faculty: "We have learnt far more from the women than we were able to teach them. The Bankura experience has coloured our entire perspective – in research, training or advocacy."

ILO team member: "The community's productive base has expanded to generate additional employment. It's noteworthy that so much government funding and support was mobilized. . . . Costs are low when you consider that it was a new model of women's advancement, and is now tested for widespread replication."

India has 175 million hectares of wasteland, a quarter of which is in private marginal holdings. The model of women's Samity-owned regeneration therefore has far-reaching implications for wasteland development. Several NGOs in Orissa, Rajasthan, Gujarat and other States have already taken steps to replicate such a model of waste-land reclamation.

INFERENCES

In a span of seven years the Bankura project has evolved from spontaneous group activity to a widespread movement of waste-land reclamation and income-generating activities, directly covering thirty-six villages in two districts. The project's unwavering focus on human advancement has both complicated and simplified its passage. The model of growth via women's organizations has remarkable potential but it also has limitations, both structural and operational. What are the project's advantages and weaknesses, who has benefited most, and what inferences may be drawn for women's development projects?

Benefits are reported by all the 1,500 members of the twelve Samities, of course in varying degrees. Estimates show that 1,500 women have supplementary employment in the local area, with a management system which women control, and therefore where employment can be predicted by the women themselves: "The Samity is an organization which gives us strength. As long as we hold on to this strength, no one can take it away from us. All are accountable to all."

The project has aroused initiative among women in adjoining blocks and districts, and large offers of land donation have been made by communities to women's groups.

There has been a notable impact on the government's delivery mechanism in the local area for schemes and programmes directed towards target groups. The Bankura model of development via managerial organizations of women at the grass roots appears to have been accepted as the preferred structure for group-based women's schemes such as DWCRA[9] but has a long way to go before affecting most routine development programmes.

With its geographical spread and deepening impact, the short-comings of the project have also become visible. Conceptually, the dependence of grass-roots groups on an intermediate agency such as the CWDS continues to be a debated point. Will CWDS's withdrawal not weaken the negotiating power of the Samities *vis-à-vis* local bodies? While there are no unambiguous answers, Samity members are already taking over several functions from the CWDS field staff. Also, CWDS will remain available later too for consultation and crisis support.

Another "flaw" is structural: the principle of freedom of association entitles an unlimited number of women to join the Samities, although each Samity has only a limited capacity to generate employment based on land regeneration or small enterprises.

There are some serious constraints in implementation, too. First, the products of many of the small enterprises are sold to government departments, which are buyers only as long as official policy on the subject does not shift: therefore the Samities are operating in a protected and vulnerable environment; second, the flow of inputs from government sources is often delayed and unpredictable – as, for instance, in the short supply of saplings for plantation; third, CWDS's lack of expertise in land and water-resource management resulted in a staffing pattern not entirely compatible with the technical needs of the project. This "flaw" has been corrected partially by associating technical consultants and experts, and by training Samity members since March 1987 in water-harvesting techniques, nursery-raising, tree species selection, crop rotation, etc.; and forth, the local staff of CWDS has a high rate of turnover due to the allurements of permanent government jobs, and these resignations jolt the CWDS field structure and Samities.

Despite these shortcomings, the obvious strength of the Bankura Samities tempts one to raise important macro-questions: on women's bargaining power; on the appropriate methodology for rural women's groups; issues around which women mobilize; self-reliance. Some general inferences do emerge, which are presented here, at the risk of oversimplification.

• Poorest rural women are motivated for group action because they regard this as the only protection against their vulnerability as individuals at work, at home and in society. CWDS stresses that "it is necessary only to find feasible methods and resources to meet their basic objectives which they state so often, but to which few people pay attention."

- Control over a productive asset such as land by a Samity increases women's bargaining power as workers, and could lead to changes in local production relations as well as power relations within the family and the community.
- Employment is an effective means of mobilization, which generates a creative environment for programmes of broader reform.
- Wasted private assets can be regenerated by local women's groups, provided ownership or usufruct of the asset vests in the group.
- A substantial amount of supplementary employment can be generated through scientific management of natural resources by women's groups, on private or public assets. The precondition is that the women's groups acquire legal ownership/usufruct of the asset. In the Bankura project, ten Samities generated 36,000 person days of direct employment for 1,200 women at about Rs. 6 per day through plantations and business ventures, besides income from stipends during training.
- The local government machinery tends to support women's groups more readily than individual women. However, government district and block officials are not always adequately informed about the provisions of different schemes for assisting women's groups, and also lack mechanisms for co-ordinating the assistance.
- The Bankura project has also found that the provisions of government schemes are often more suited to the needs of the official staff than to those of the women. For instance, government training facilities seem to be organized to suit the trainers, not the trainees. Equally the Bankura experience also reveals that although training and assistance schemes seem to be designed for educated individuals, they can be recast to suit the requirement of rural women who are largely illiterate.
- The project confirms that group-based activities like those of the Bankura project can be funded via government schemes – ranging from training, to labour wages for plantations, group businesses, infrastructural support (e.g. veterinary cover, tassar

egg supply) and materials (e.g. cement, kitchen garden tools from the BDO).

- The project also demonstrates how, over time, government programmes can get welded into women's groups for instance, via the appointment of Samity members as Anganwadi supervisors.
- Government's ability to modify its approach and update understanding is evidenced from the fact that CWDS organizers and Samity members have been called upon to train social forestry officials and managers of specific schemes such as DWCRA. Officials who have taken part in these programmes say admiringly: "When many women in torn saris come together, and speak so pertinently and forcefully they radiate a sense of power and authority. You *have* to take note of what they're saying."
- Relatively big grass-roots organizations show a resoluteness of purpose which counters pressures from outside, and internal frustration, as for instance at a delay in employment creation. Smaller groups are initially more susceptible to "interference" from village power groups.
- Women's grass-roots organizations can be made more effective in the long term if they are institutionally linked to local bodies, both elected and official, because the community acknowledges these structures of power. Illustratively, the Bankura Samities are affiliated with the WBTDCC, LAMPS, and some Samity women have been elected to the local Panchayat.
- Women's groups tend to remain essentially non-political, although they encourage their members to contest local election (on the individual basis, many women belong to political parties). Parties try to co-opt these organizations, especially at election time, but this has to be resisted to prevent any scope for disruptive manipulation.
- The informal-within-formal structure of the women's groups, and participation in activities which yield income and enhance general life quality, appear to promote an improved self-image, which in turn increases bargaining power.
- Family and community accept women's groups when women gain financially, and general environmental changes are visible.

203

- Success of an innovative project seems to depend on person-
alities, whether at the village level or at the "intellectual"
headquarters. Equally, untapped reservoirs of leadership exist
both at the village level and amongst organizational cadres.

The Bankura project seems to answer some of the macro-questions
raised earlier. On the appropriate methodology for rural women's
advancement, the project points to the effective action possibilities
generated by women's own groups utilizing local natural resources
and funded through existing government schemes. On the issue of
bargaining power, the experience shows that a Samity's control over
a productive asset such as an arjun plantation increases women
members' potential to negotiate wages in the local labour market,
and this could possibly lead to a change in local production relations
if the Samity owns a sufficiently large amount of land. On the
stabilizing mechanism for local women's groups, the project points
to the significant role of an intermediate organization such as the
CWDS, which has analytical clarity regarding the women's question,
and *locus standi* in decision-making bodies. It also shows that
community approval is forthcoming if the activities bring common
gain. *Is self-reliance of a women's group necessary?* The project
has provided no clear answers. Vinadi is opposed to imposing
self-reliance prematurely: "When self-reliance is not tested as an
indicator of economic growth where modernization of the economy
is under discussion, then why should it become the most important
indicator for measuring rural women's efforts to expand their world
through participation?"

What is the Samities' future?

Samities have received more offers of land, and are now exploring
the feasibility of other land-based activities. Perhaps they will use
the new patches to create village woodlots or raise mixed plantations
with fodder, fuel, fruit, or house-building materials. Enterprises for
individual women will certainly increase as their collective resources
grow and enhance their revolving funds.

As a natural sequel to the momentum generated by the existing Samities, new Samities are being formed and others are under discussion in two adjacent districts, Purulia and Medinipur.
They might evolve new land-use patterns, and a new set of

activities, both for women's groups and for individual members.

CWDS has already changed its original decision to confine the project to one block. Will it move to the adjacent district, or will another intermediate agency step in? Perhaps both events will occur, and eventually intermediate agencies might be redundant. "CWDS will withdraw when women are inducted in substantial numbers into the local Panchayats, and they become effective decision-makers. Then the Panchayat will lobby for the Samities, and stand by them. We see that happening already."

Bankura women are in control of their future, and they are not daunted by the fact that finally they will be wholly responsible for themselves.

"We have learnt that actually it is the land that owns the people. We have worked hard to give the land a green cover, and in return it has clothed us with authority. We are advancing together. The journey has begun."

NOTES

1. Smallest administrative unit, composed of an average of 75 to 100 villages, with a total population of about 125,000.
2. Rural Women Workers' Advancement Society.
3. AFPRO: Action for Food Production, a voluntary agency which specializes in technical aspects of land and water resource management.
4. Panchayat: Elected village committee, usually covering three to five villages.
5. Panchayat Samiti and Zila Parishad: Elected people's institutions at Block and district level, respectively.
6. Gramin Melas: village fairs, which are usually traditional trade fairs, specializing in, for instance, animals or agricultural produce.
7. Kisan: farmer.
8. DANIDA: Danish Development Agency.
9. DWCRA: Development of Women and Children in Rural Areas, a scheme of the government of India partially supported by UNICEF.